Black and White Sat Down Together

Mary White Ovington in her youth.

Black and White Sat Down Together

The Reminiscences of an NAACP Founder

Mary White Ovington

Edited and with a Foreword by
Ralph E. Luker
Afterword by Carolyn E. Wedin

The Feminist Press
at The City University of New York
New York

Published 1995 by The Feminist Press at The City University of New York
311 East 94 Street, New York, NY 10128-5684

First paperback edition 1996

Mary White Ovington's "Reminiscences" were serially published in the *Baltimore Afro-American*, September 1932 through February 1933. The editor of this volume has corrected typographical errors in the original and has made adjustments to punctuation.

02 01 00 99 98 97 96   5 4 3 2 1

Library of Congress Cataloging-in-Publication Data

Ovington, Mary White, 1865–1951.
  Black and White Sat Down Together: the reminiscences of an NAACP
  founder / Mary White Ovington; edited and with a foreword by
  Ralph E. Luker; afterword by Carolyn Wedin.
    p.   cm.
  Includes biographical references (p.)
  ISBN 1-55861-099-5 (cloth)
  ISBN 1-55861-156-8 (pbk)
    1. Ovington, Mary White, 1865–1951. 2. Afro-Americans—Biography.
3. National Association for the Advancement of Colored People—Biography.   4. Civil rights
workers—United States—Biography.
5. Afro-Americans—Civil Rights. 6. Civil rights movements—United States—History—20th
century. I. Luker, Ralph. II. Title
  E185.97.O95A3 1995
  323.1'196073'092-dc20
  [B]   94-41363
                                                CIP

This publication is made possible, in part, by public funds from the New York State Council on the Arts. The Feminist Press is also grateful to Mariam K. Chamberlain, Helene D. Goldfarb, Joanne Markell, Rubie Saunders, Caroline Urvater, and Genevieve Vaughan for their generosity.

Cover photo of Mary White Ovington courtesy of Photographs and Prints Division, Schomburg Center for Research in Black Culture, The New York Public Library, Astor, Lenox, and Tilden Foundations.
Text design by Paula Martinac

Typeset by Stanton Publications Services, St. Paul, Minnesota
Printed in the United States of America on acid-free paper by
McNaughton & Gunn, Inc., Saline, Michigan

Contents

Foreword

Twelve years ago, while doing research for a book on racial reform in the late nineteenth and early twentieth centuries, I found references to and ultimately examined Mary White Ovington's "Reminiscences, or Going Back 40 Years," which had been published fifty years earlier in the *Baltimore Afro-American*, from 17 September 1932 through 25 February 1933. Her recollections of forty years of experience in race relations deserved a wider audience, I thought. Working from blurred, nearly blinding, copies of text from negative microfilm (the irony of "white over black" was not lost on me), I transcribed Ovington's weekly installments into my computer and sent the manuscript to several publishers. Ultimately, Florence Howe of The Feminist Press shared my enthusiasm for recovering the experience of Mary White Ovington. Later, working from copies of the *Afro-American*'s republication of the "Reminiscences" in 1951 and 1952, Carolyn Wedin helped by correcting typesetting mistakes in the earlier newspaper copy and transcription errors resulting from blurred or obscure text. Susannah Driver and sharp-eyed readers for The Feminist Press saved me from egregious errors. In the interest of clarity and because Ovington's "Reminiscences" were published in varying newspaper forms, we agreed that spelling and typesetting errors would be silently corrected or standardized without the constant repetition of *sic*.

Ralph E. Luker

Chronology

1865	Mary White Ovington is born in Brooklyn, New York, on April 11.
1888–91	Attends Packer Collegiate Institute.
1890	Hears Frederick Douglass speak at Brooklyn's Plymouth Church.
1891–3	Attends Radcliffe College.
1893–4	Registrar at Brooklyn's Pratt Institute.
1895	Helps to found Pratt Institute's Greenpoint Settlement in Brooklyn.
1896–1903	Head worker at Greenpoint Settlement.
1900	Tours London's East End slums.
	New York experiences its worst race riot since the Civil War.
1903	Hears Booker T. Washington speak at the Social Reform Club in Manhattan.

W.E.B. Du Bois publishes *The Souls of Black Folk*.

1903–4   Ovington develops typhoid fever; while convalescing, travels in Italy and makes her first trip to the South, visiting Hampton Institute, where she meets W.E.B. Du Bois.

Fellow in social work at Mary Kingsbury Simkhovitch's Greenwich House in Manhattan; begins her study of employment and housing problems in black Manhattan.

1904–9   Works with two New York organizations, the National League for the Protection of Colored Women and the Committee for Improving the Industrial Condition of Negroes in New York, which merge in 1911 to become the National Urban League.

1905   Joins the Socialist Party.

1906   Covers meetings of Washington's National Negro Business League in Atlanta and Du Bois's Niagara Movement at Harper's Ferry, West Virginia, for Oswald Garrison Villard's *New York Post*.

Three months after Ovington's visit, Atlanta experiences a severe race riot.

1906–7	During the winter, Ovington makes her first extended tour of the South, visiting Atlanta and several communities in Alabama.
1908	Moves into Manhattan's Tuskegee Apartments, becoming the model tenement's sole white resident.
	Lurid newspaper accounts of Ovington's participation in the Cosmopolitan Club's multiracial dinner generates hostile mail.
	Springfield, Illinois, has a severe race riot, which leads Ovington, William English Walling, Oswald Garrison Villard and others to call for a national conference on racial justice.
1909	Ovington's father dies.
	The National Conference on the Negro meets in New York to organize the National Negro Committee.
1910	Ovington and her mother spend February and March in Jamaica.
	The second National Negro Conference meets in New York to adopt an organizational structure and a name, the National Association for the Advancement of Colored People.

Du Bois joins the NAACP staff as Director of Publicity and Research.

1910–11   Ovington serves briefly as acting Executive Secretary of the NAACP.

1911   Ovington publishes her study of black Manhattan, *Half a Man*.

Attends the Universal Races Congress in London and tours the continent.

1912   Woodrow Wilson is elected President of the United States. During his eight years in office, racial segregation becomes policy in federal offices.

1913   Ovington publishes *Hazel*, a novel for children, and "The Status of the Negro in the United States" in the *New Review*.

1914   "Socialism and the Feminist Movement" published in the *New Review*.

Oswald Garrison Villard resigns as Chairman of the NAACP's Board of Directors.

1915   D. W. Griffith's "Birth of a Nation" premiers in California. The NAACP protests its showing across the nation for years thereafter.

1916   Ovington publishes "Mary Phagan Speaks" in the *New Republic* and "The White Brute" in the *New Masses*.

           Joel E. Spingarn resigns as Chairman of the NAACP's Board of Directors.

           Ovington publishes "The United States in Porto Rico" in the *New Republic*.

1917   The United States enters World War I.

1918   John R. Shillady becomes Executive Secretary of the NAACP.

1919   Ovington becomes Chairman of the NAACP's Board of Directors.

           The NAACP publishes *Thirty Years of Lynching in the United States, 1889–1918*, a major contribution to its crusade against lynching.

           Shillady is beaten in Austin, Texas.

           Ovington publishes *The Shadow*, a novel of mistaken racial identity, and *The Upward Path*, an anthology for black children.

           James Weldon Johnson becomes the NAACP's Executive Secretary, the first African American to hold the position.

For the first time, the NAACP holds its national convention in the South, in Atlanta.

Ovington travels across the country to attend the National Association of Colored Women's convention in Denver.

1921   Begins a book review column, "Book Chat," which focuses on racial literature.

Tours the West Coast on behalf of the NAACP.

1923   Publishes *The Awakening*, a play.

Persuades the NAACP to focus its attention on winning equal dollars for black school systems in the South.

1927   Publishes *Portraits in Color*, biographical sketches of prominent African Americans.

Ovington's mother dies.

1930   The NAACP successfully lobbies for the defeat of John J. Parker's nomination to the United States Supreme Court.

James Weldon Johnson resigns as NAACP Executive Secretary.

1931   Ovington publishes *Zeke*, a children's novel.

Walter White becomes the NAACP's Executive Secretary.

1932   Ovington publishes *Phillis Wheatley*, a play.

Resigns as Chairman of the NAACP's Board of Directors and becomes its Treasurer.

1932–33   Publishes her "Reminiscences" in the *Baltimore Afro-American*.

1934   After Du Bois espouses "voluntary segregation," Walter White and others force his resignation from NAACP office.

1939   The NAACP's Legal Defense and Educational Fund is incorporated as a tax-exempt corporation to carry on the NAACP's civil rights litigation and education programs, but to operate independently of the parent organization.

1940   Although active in policy debates through the 1930s, Ovington is increasingly inactive thereafter.

1947   Publishes *The Walls Came Tumbling Down*, a popular history of the NAACP.

                       Resigns as Treasurer of the NAACP.

1951   Ovington dies in Auburndale, Massachusetts.

1951–2   The *Baltimore Afro-American* re-publishes "Reminiscences."

Preface

$\mathcal{I}$n one of his early essays, Du Bois finds that the white man, under his polite talk, is always thinking the question, "What does it mean to be a problem?"

I have found since I have become known in radical Negro work that colored people, under their pleasant greetings, are thinking, "Why did you take up the Negro cause?" Indeed, as the question is in no way embarrassing to me, they sometimes ask it. I try to answer, but it takes a long time to explain. One thing after another occurs to me as a contributory reason. And in the effort to answer this question I find myself reviewing my many years of Negro work. So I have written this story that will take nearly half a year of the *Afro-American*'s weekly issues.

It will deal with my work, with controversial matters, will talk frankly of colored people as well as of white. Before this I have had an eye on educating the white world. These reminiscences are not meant to educate anybody. They are what I think important bits out of a portion of my life of thought and action. The editor of the *Afro-American* believes they will interest you. If the questions asked by people all over the country are a criterion, I believe he is right. So my reminiscences begin.

Early Impressions

The time is 1890. Two young people are walking down Fulton Street, Brooklyn. The girl, in long winter coat, slips her hand into the man's arm. When night comes this is etiquette in a city inadequately lighted. The girl is conspicuously blonde, blue eyes, pink cheeks, golden hair; the man—well, if you want to know what the man looked like, see McMonnies's statue of Nathan Hale in the New York City Hall Park. He posed for it, and it's a perfect likeness.

The couple turn down Orange Street to Plymouth Church. They are going to a lecture by Frederick Douglass, who recently, against the advice of his oldest friends, married a white woman. He gave his explanation to a mixed audience in Atlanta: "My father was white; my mother was black. My first wife was black; my second wife is white. I have paid my respects to both my parents." The two young people are arguing excitedly on this matter. The girl is of New York and Yankee descent. The young man, she realizes for the first time, has roots in Baltimore.

"How could she do it?" the young man says.

"If she wanted to, she had a right to," the girl persists. "It is a personal matter."

But this is what the man will not accept for a moment, and, still arguing, the one in defense of the dominant race, the other in defense of the individual, they enter the church.

They sit in the gallery almost over the platform. The meeting-house that, under Beecher's leadership, has heard many anti-slavery speeches, is filled with expectant people. The organ plays "John Brown's Body" and Douglass mounts the platform.

He is a strong, powerfully built man, with brown skin and a shock of bushy hair. His eyes gleam with that liveliness to things about him so common to the Negro. He stands at the reading desk, immovable, unsmiling, looking at the applauding audience. The girl

3

leans forward, clapping excitedly. The man leans forward, too, and pays his tribute.

"I don't wonder she married him," he says. "He looks like Aesop."

I had never seen Frederick Douglass before (I drop the third person not to resume it) and I was never to see him again, but that night was to me a great event. I had come face to face with one of my heroes. To my companion, who had always thought of the Negro as a servant, this unknown colored man was a revelation, but I had heard of him since I could remember. He was coupled with Garrison in my excited thoughts. In imagination I had seen him, after his perilous journey by train and boat, set foot on free soil in Philadelphia, and I had followed him as he preached against slavery in the North and in England. He was one of the great group of men and women who had risked all for freedom.

Here I think was the great difference not only between my attitude and that of my friend, but between my attitude and the attitude of all Southerners and most Northerners. If they knew the Negro at all they knew him as a servant. I did not know the Negro in the flesh. My "mammy" was Irish and quite as devoted, I am sure, as any black woman. We had no Negro servants. Once a year at Thanksgiving time, an old, blind Negro, led by an attractive boy, came to our church and asked for money for the Howard Orphan Asylum. I think we sent him away pleased. Anyway, he always said so. He was the only Negro with whom I had any contact. Otherwise, I knew the race by its heroic deeds.

The Southerner feels that this proves his thesis and that he, not I, knew the Negro. But is he right? There are people and nations whom we know that we have never seen. We have not seen Leonidas at Thermopylae or listened to Spartacus. But we know the Greek and the Roman better by reading their history than by confining ourselves to the acquaintanceship of the florists and fruit venders who come to us from Greece and Italy. I read the story of the slave in his insurrections and his escapes from serfdom, in Harriet Tubman and Frederick Douglass, in Box Brown and Anthony Burns and a host of others. This heroic side of slavery the South hated and feared and denied. So I maintained that I did know the Negro because I knew the possibilities of heroism in the race. "The highest is the measure of the man" was said by a white man and is accepted for white men. It should also be accepted for the Negro.

Ours was an abolition family. My grandmother on my mother's side came from Brooklyn, Connecticut, where, as a young girl, she was under the preaching of Samuel J. May. He helped her to the highest ideals. I was with her when she died and heard her in her last words repeat his benediction: "Help us to be more pure and holy, more devout and thankful, more heartily inclined to every good work." His good works included complete devotion to the anti-slavery cause. His disciple was not an aggressive woman, but she went to anti-slavery meetings and told me of the mobs she had encountered. I was a sympathetic listener.

My father left Plymouth Church because Beecher had dealings with the foreign missionary association that in turn had dealings with the slaveholder. That is as I remember it. He joined the Unitarian Church, in which my mother had been reared, and sat under Samuel Longfellow, whose abolitionism was of the strictest brand. And the minister, John White Chadwick, who came to our little Unitarian Church shortly after I was born, was always a radical on the Negro question. He used to lecture on some of the great Americans and taught us to despise Daniel Webster for his Fourth of March speech and Henry Clay for his continual compromising. George Williams Curtis often lectured for us, and I can remember his description of how "Henry Clay, compromise incarnate, left the Senate when Charles Sumner, conscience incarnate, entered it." Garrison was a personal friend of my grandmother (his wife came from Brooklyn, Connecticut) and was my childhood's greatest hero, with Robert Bruce as a close second. I knew how he was dragged through the streets of Boston by the mob.

We spent our summers in the country, at quiet places, usually on a hilltop. I had a passion for the starlight. Evenings were never a problem, for if nothing was going on at the little boarding-house, there was always the open road and the stars. The few horse-drawn vehicles that went by were negligible. So I could study the constellations undisturbed. Emerson said, "If the stars should appear one night in a thousand years how men would worship and adore and preserve for generations the memory of the City of God that had been shown." For three months this City of God was spread before me, save for the nights when it was blotted out by the rain.

The North Star I cared for most. It embodied heroism. I saw the slave creep through the swamp, his clothes ragged, his feet bare. I saw him reach Canada. I always felt ashamed that complete safety only came outside the borders of the United States.

I was a happy, healthy child, playing hard and enjoying school to the utmost. I was taught by a family of great teachers. But, being sensitive, this abolition teaching made a deep impression upon me. However, I never thought of going out into action. The economic depression of Reconstruction, like the economic depression today, monopolized men's emotions. At home I never heard of any work for the emancipated slave. Even my minister took little interest in Negro education. Slavery was ended. That was the great point. The Thirteenth, Fourteenth, and Fifteenth Amendments had been passed. The Negro was free and a citizen. These two facts cast everything else in the shade. So when, after a leisurely private school education, two years at Radcliffe College, and three years of what we called "going into society," I turned to earn my living, I never thought of the Negro. Instead, I went among white working-class people and started a settlement in my own city. But that's a story for another chapter.

17 September 1932

Settlement Work

$\mathcal{I}$n my youth, and it is partly true today, no place was more remote than that section of the city in which persons of a different caste lived. I was born and reared on Brooklyn Heights. When Frederick B. Pratt of Pratt Institute (where, after leaving college, I spent a year in a secretarial position) asked me to look at a model tenement his family had built in northern Brooklyn to see if it offered possibilities for settlement work, he sent me to an unknown land.

The Astral, as it was called, was one of the first model tenements erected in Greater New York. It was in Greenpoint, the northernmost ward of Brooklyn. To get there I took a car that I had seen all my life but never entered, went for a couple of miles through familiar streets, and then explored the unknown.

Sugar refineries gave out their sickish smell, factories loomed large, and at length Greenpoint was reached, ugly but within view of the river. I climbed four flights of tenement stairs and knocked at the door of an apartment where a girl from Minneapolis had been living while working in the Pratt library.

In an hour she told me of conditions in our own city of which I was utterly ignorant. I felt humiliated and decided to take up the settlement job. Since then I have played the role of the Minneapolis girl in Southern towns, talking with my Southern white friends and telling them of the well-to-do Negro. They are never humiliated. They always know all they want to know.

There was a fervor for settlement work in the nineties, for learning working-class conditions by living among the workers and sharing, to a small extent, in their lives. Toynbee Hall, London, Hull House, Greenwich House, the Henry Street Settlement, these were a few familiar names. My little plant grew from five rooms to forty, occupying a section in the model tenement, but it never achieved fame. Pratt Institute largely furnished the teachers, making it a prac-

7

tice station for students in domestic science. The Institute and the Pratt family generously raised the money.

I had no serious financial care and was happy in a growing family of residents and in the many contacts such work gave. I knew Jane Addams and have never forgotten her first piece of advice to me: "If you want to be surrounded by second-rate ability, you will dominate your settlement. If you want the best ability, you must allow great liberty of action among your residents."

Jane Addams's name today is among the most famous in the world. But perhaps few people realize the incalculable good she has done in helping others to enlarge and glorify their own work. Many people can build their fortune by using others. Few can encourage ability without dominating it.

We worked hard at the Greenpoint Settlement, and we tried to understand working-class conditions. The desire for such knowledge was in the air.

New York had then the Social Reform Club, an organization comprising a membership of intellectuals and workers. I entered it and was soon put upon its board. I was lucky to begin my work at a time when hope was in the air, not when, as today, the atmosphere reeks with the philosophy of economic and psychological collapse.

We believed in political reform and elected Seth Low mayor. We had a tenement house department that abolished the building of dark, almost windowless tenements. We talked socialism and single tax and when we read William Morris, or sang his hymn of the workers at the Intercollegiate Socialist Society, we believed that by sacrifice and hard work his dream might come true.

With this background I worked in the Greenpoint Settlement for seven years.

How much I helped the neighborhood I do not know, not a great deal, but I learned much myself. Numbers of factory girls came to our classes and when I heard the whistle blow at seven in the morning, as I lay in bed, it was not an indefinite person but Mary or Amanda or Celia, who was going to do rough work for ten and a half hours.

A few children were then in the mills, and I saw one with mangled hand who had no excuse for what she had done except that she was so much a child she wanted to play with machinery. I saw the struggle for jobs, the boycott, and the tragedy of the unemployed. And I saw happy children.

For the children, with whom we did much of our work, on the whole were happy. They loved the street and its excitement. Usually, they had enough to eat and a place to sleep. They came from families of industrious people, chiefly Irish and German Americans, went to public school, learned a little, and were up to mischief in their leisure hours.

The boys stole lead pipes, climbed everywhere, walking along the outside coping of our seven-story tenement, brought the cooking teacher to me in tears because they had begun by eating up all the raw material for the lesson except the salt, in short, were very genuine American toughs, bad but lovable. When they got their working papers and began to earn something, they settled down to respectable life. Some have done well. One went to Congress. Perhaps I should add, one went to jail.

The girls were not so restless, and soon learned to wheel baby carriages or hold a toddler by the arm.

It seemed to me the old suffered most. So little could be done for them! A grandmother needs an armchair and a pleasant window. Our grandmothers huddled in corners, the horror of the poorhouse hanging over them. The mothers, too, were often sad and tired. Some of the men drank, and there was nothing attractive about their drunkenness, but many were hard working and I used to wonder what they could get out of life, their homes were so crowded and noisy. Neither the movie nor the radio had been invented.

That I should later work for the Negro never entered my mind, but I doubt if I could have had a better preparation than the settlement gave. For in those seven years I learned that many problems attributed to race are really labor problems.

Employers of labor, whether men or women, employing white or black, have a good deal the same psychology, talk in much the same way. The domestic service problem takes on local color, but the mistresses always think the same thing—that a good servant neglects her own people for her mistress.

I did, however, have two direct contacts with Negro life while at Greenpoint, and one of them, more than any other single thing, led me to take up colored work.

The first was the attitude of the boys in our clubs toward the colored population. I encountered it when I took a club to Prospect Park. Our route lay through a small Negro section, Gwinnett Street, a block or two of old frame houses occupied by the poorer class. (Once, one of the most beautiful girls I have ever seen in my life got on the car at Gwinnett Street. She was tall and slender and dressed in golden brown corduroy that made her brown skin glow with lovely color.)

The families were sitting on their stoops, and, as we passed them, as though at a signal, all the boys jumped on their seats and at the tops of their voices shouted: "Nigger, nigger, nigger!" Then, as the car turned into a white neighborhood, they sat down. The game was over.

They never played it again with me, but I carried my will by threat rather than persuasion. They saw no harm in what they did.

As time went on, I realized there was no personal animosity in their act. It was a custom. When a colored janitor, oddly enough named George, came to take charge of our model tenement, he became the most popular man among the boys on the block. There was always a group about him, listening to his stories. He was an individual to them.

My second direct Negro contact was through the Social Reform Club. "Up From Slavery" was appearing in the *Outlook* and our club wanted to honor the author of it and his wife. (They were disappointed when the wife proved to be number three, not number two about whom they were reading.) I was made chairman of the committee to arrange for the dinner.

"Do not have all the talk about conditions in the South. Have conditions in the North discussed."

These were my instructions and I followed them. To my amazement I learned that there was a Negro problem in my city. I had honestly never thought of it. I accepted the Negro as I accepted any other element in the population. That he suffered more from poverty, from segregation, from prejudice, than any other race in the city was a new idea to me. The educated, well-to-do Negro was also discussed and criticized, gently, for not standing up more for his rights.

Booker Washington did not shine particularly that night. Maggie Washington made an interesting speech on her work among Negro mothers. But the person who remains in my memory is the late William H. Baldwin. I can see him now at the speakers' table, leaning forward, looking at Washington, and saying: "I worship that man."

I went home with a new idea. I was considering leaving Greenpoint. Our work was growing less important since the public school system had started evening classes in domestic science. Might not my next venture be among Negroes?

That was my last year at Greenpoint. I left more of a radical than when I entered. Labor conditions about me and the discussions at the Social Reform Club had made me a Socialist, though I did not join the party for two years. I was more revolutionary than the workers with whom I came in contact. It was hard to get them even to agitate for shorter hours. They were afraid of losing their jobs.

The well fed, whose jobs are not precarious, can agitate for the poor. But let their jobs be touched and they are as conservative as anyone else. John Bright worked for the improvement of the rural laborer in England, but his father's money was in industry and the son never helped the factory hand.

Greenpoint seems far away now. I have kept up with a few of my boys and girls, but I never go back. Another race, another group, has absorbed my attention. I learned a lot living among working people, but I doubt whether I did much except for a few individuals.

I could not change the economic situation, and the things for which I cared most Greenpoint did not care for at all. Books were too dull to open. Music, in any real sense, was unknown. There were glorious exceptions, but the intellectual stimulation that a Jewish neighborhood gives was unknown to me.

I shall never forget the first party the boys gave and to which I was invited as an honored guest. I spent my time watching the hands of the great clock on the wall move slowly, so slowly that each minute was ten. Any second I expected a trustee to enter and view the horrid vaudeville.

I gave a party in return that soon got quite beyond my control. The girls sat in the boys' laps, explaining to me afterwards that there were not chairs enough to go around. Of cake and fruit, thrown playfully about, there was gathered up afterwards one large pailful. The dancing class was formed to teach manners. It helped, but much, very much was left to be desired.

While I swept up the floor after a party I consoled myself with the thought that this would all change with the coming generation. The children of these boys and girls, with improved industrial conditions, with shorter hours, would love the finest things in life. The shorter hours have come but not the dream. Indeed, the reverse has occurred.

Instead of Greenpoint's reaching up to the polite elevation of Brooklyn Heights, it has pulled the old elevation down amid laughter and jeers.

24 September 1932

I Begin My Investigation

The summer after I left Greenpoint I had my one serious illness, typhoid. It took nearly a year for recovery. A trip to Italy came in the spring, and it was not until the following autumn, 1904, that I was at work again.

The desire to have a settlement among the Negroes had been mulling in my mind for these months. I felt that a settlement in a Negro section would not only help the poor but would be an excellent meeting-place for the well-to-do of each race.

Here, on the equality that I knew could exist in a settlement, white and colored could live together, and race questions would not be the only matters under discussion. But I had never had to raise money and I was at a loss how to begin to interest people. So I went to one of my wisest settlement friends, Mary Kingsbury Simkhovitch, head of Greenwich House, and asked her advice. She in her turn asked me what I knew of Negro conditions.

I confessed that I knew nothing. Whereupon she advised that I study the Negro in New York and made this practical by securing a fellowship for me from Greenwich House. This resulted in the publication of my book, in 1911, by Longmans, Green, *Half a Man: The Status of the Negro in New York*.

I wanted first to meet the educated Negro, but I had not a single acquaintance. Once, on revisiting Radcliffe, I was disappointed at seeing a colored girl in the library and realizing that I had lost this natural way of meeting the colored world. However, I didn't know even one college girl, so I had to use letters of introduction from Washington and Du Bois. I mailed ten to prominent business men asking for interviews.

I learned the meaning of CPT! Fred Moore, editor of the New York *Age*, answered by return mail. The others took their time. One took two weeks, another six weeks. Four never answered at all. All were cordial when later I met them one by one. But, as business

13

men, according to the standard of the white world around them, they failed on the first count. They did not promptly attend to their morning mail.

Mr. Moore was helpful and I was glad to get the viewpoint of an enthusiastic Washingtonian. I was already a Du Bois enthusiast, having read his articles in the *Atlantic Monthly* that were later incorporated in *The Souls of Black Folk*. Business proved one of the least interesting phases to study.

The Negro had been steadily losing out since the days when he constituted ten percent of the city's population—a few men in real estate, a few caterers, some small shops, seemed all. One man did impress me. Wallace of Virginia, labor leader and head of the Asphalt Workers' Union. I saw him at the Sunday afternoon labor gathering, a dark man, speaking to the point, business-like. He handled more Italians than Negroes. His trade, however, was soon to be doomed.

My efforts to meet the professional class were more successful. As a social worker, I at once studied the social service work for the Negroes. There was the Friends' Mission, under white guidance, down in the West Thirties. Mrs. Kimber, calm, benignant, was at the head, and with her a young girl, Kate Sherman, as enthusiastic as ever I could hope to be. I remember her saying once, "My heart is black, even though my face may be white." She showed me some shocking conditions, but she knew few Negroes of her own calibre.

Soon I became acquainted with the colored nurses connected with the Henry Street Settlement and the Bureau of Charities and also with the members of the mixed boards of the Walton Free Kindergarten and the Hope Day Nursery. The colored churches gave me welcome. I became familiar with the all too small group of philanthropic workers. To mention names would take too long and would be interesting only to old New Yorkers. But I want my readers to understand that I earnestly tried to look at New York's Negro problem from the various angles that the Negroes themselves looked at it. I have met many white people, North as well as South, who, knowing one Negro whom they like, base their philanthropy upon his advice.

I met a New York man not so long ago who had raised nearly a hundred thousand dollars for a Negro without inquiring how he stood with his own group. I was blamed for not endorsing him and not using my influence to get the Negroes to endorse. I was to take the Negro on this white man's evaluation. All very pleasant for the white man, but there are Mussolinis enough of the Negro's making without the white man's manufacturing more.

Through the social workers I met the professional people. They were a pleasant, friendly group with nothing to distinguish them from their neighbors but their color. Most of them lived in houses in Brooklyn which they owned and which were a little more ugly in a solid, mid-Victorian way than the whites. Whether Northerners or Southerners, they were usually descendants of free men and had been well educated by their parents.

What most impressed me was their conservatism—not on the race question but on everything else. They saw the white man given opportunities denied them, and they wanted the status of the white man to be able to go where their money would take them. Engrossed by their own problem, they did not take up the problems of others. In politics they were Republicans.

Maritcha Lyons, since deceased, was one of the most attractive of this group. She won the right of colored graduates from the normal college to teach in the public schools. Few outside of New York know that there is no discrimination in the placing of colored normal graduates and that they frequently teach in schools where there are no Negroes. I went to Superintendent Maxwell when I began my investigations and asked him for a list of colored teachers. He gave me to understand from his manner that my question was an impertinence. Teachers were put into schools without regard to their color. He did not know how many colored teachers he had nor where they were teaching.

While superintendent, Maxwell held rigidly to this rule. But before his time the colored women had gained the point he emphasized. The Negro had worked and suffered to gain what he has in New York City.

As I look through the mass of letters that I have kept, I see how unendingly kind my new acquaintances were to me. Busy ministers gave me interviews and helped me to meet people who could tell me more. I have had the privilege of the Reverend Hutchins Bishop's friendship for over thirty years. I went from one denomination to another in my quest for knowledge.

The late William H. Brooks of St. Mark's told me that his study door was always open. We had a disagreement on the Roosevelt-Washington dinner, I believing Washington was right in accepting the hospitality.

Dr. Brooks wrote me his idea on the matter: "Mr. Roosevelt had a right to invite Mr. Washington. Mr. Washington had the right to accept. But is it the best and highest wisdom or the finest taste to make our friends suffer because it is in our power to do so?"

Reading these lines after twenty-seven years, I appreciate how many times my friends have shown the finest taste in not letting me suffer. I had a sense of adventure in going where my race did not go, where I was warned not to go. But I was not allowed to be indiscreet. I was quietly taken care of, then and always.

At the end of a Negro meeting, I went home alone or with a colored woman. Once this did not happen. I was walking in the evening with a college student. We went by a hack stand in charge of an elderly Negro. "You stop this," he said sternly to the young man. "Stop it." I had too little knowledge then to see the lynching back in his imagination, but I saw the place in which he put me.

While the professional class was on the whole conservative, there were some with a wide outlook on conditions, and before long we had a group, meeting for the most part in Brooklyn, of colored and white, called the Cosmopolitan Club. Andre Tridon, Frenchman, psychiatrist, was the president. Dr. Owen M. Waller, an able physician, an ardent admirer of Dr. Du Bois, was vice president. Dr. Verina Morton-Jones was in the club, and one of its best members was the Reverend Frazier Miller, soon to join the Socialist cause. Among the whites were single taxers and, of course, Socialists. We expected to discuss many topics, but before the evening was over we always got around to the problem of race.

I recall one evening when we examined photographs of families that lived, some in the white, some in the colored world. I had heard of these things, but it was a different matter to see pictures of Negroes who had gone white, especially when a brother, still in the colored world, exhibited them.

Southern legislatures were at that time passing laws to make a person with a drop of Negro blood a member of the Negro race. Tragic conditions were resulting.

South Carolina had refused to pass this law, a member of the legislature (I give this story as it was told me) rising and saying that they could not possibly have such legislation in that state. "We are all of us niggers, more or less," was printed from his speech in the next morning's paper.

The club was small and congenial. Later it achieved sudden fame and, as suddenly, oblivion.

While I was making social contacts, I was reading continually on the Negro question. Such reading as it was! The newspapers and magazines, with a few exceptions, had no use for any educated Negro except Booker T. Washington. He knew that the Negro should receive an industrial education and his remarks were always welcome. As the South had formerly been sensitive to Northern criticism, so now the North was ready to atone for its Reconstruction policy. The South knew all about the Negro and the North nothing.

Tourgée's *Fool's Errand* was superseded by Dixon's *Leopard's Spots*. The best publishers seemed eager to print rabid criticism of the American Negro.

Thomas, a renegade Negro, published as nasty a book as can be found about his race, and Macmillan published it. Back in the minds of the white critics was the fear of Negro domination, and the old slavery arguments were continually used. Biologically, the Negro was inferior.

Smith, of Tulane University, wrote a book to show the horrible danger of amalgamation, or, rather, of intermarriage. He assured his readers that, craniologically and by six thousand years of planet-wide experimentation (a good fundamentalist, Professor Smith), the Negro is proved to be markedly inferior to the Caucasian. He added that, if the best Negro was shown to be equal to the best Caucasian, then it would be hard to prove that the lowest white was higher than the lowest black.

A Dr. Bean of Baltimore showed to his own satisfaction that the Negro brain was smaller than the white brain and gave minute particulars regarding the different classes of American Negroes and where they came from in Africa. I sent him two pages of eager but ironic questions that asked the number of years he had spent in Africa, how long a period he had given to detailed study of the American Negro, etc., etc. He had not sallied far from Baltimore. His researches on the brain were in a few years proved incorrect. But the publication of derogatory articles went steadily on. The public wanted them.

I jumped into this world of writing and tried to get my favorable material published. The popular magazines turned it down, but *Charities* (now the *Survey*), the *Independent,* then under Ward, and the *Evening Post* published it. A number of religious journals also occasionally put in a kind word for the educated Negro. I remember, too, when the *Century* gave me a page in which I explained that the colored "mammy" existed now, as always, but that today she was mothering her own race.

I dropped into an exciting, busy world. The race question afforded me interesting contacts among whites as well as colored. Oswald Garrison Villard, Garrison's grandson, helped me unstintingly. The first time I went to him I was horrified at the way an evening meeting I had just attended had been reported. It had been a quiet, dignified affair, but the reporter described cruel vituperation against Washington, loud cries of wrath from his supporters, and a riot.

I didn't know meetings could be reported like that, but Mr. Villard did. He printed a correct report in the *Evening Post,* and I traced down the reporter from the news syndicate. That a white person should care how a Negro meeting was reported seemed amusing to the young man. I was given reporting for the *Evening Post* after this and enjoyed it hugely.

Ray Stannard Baker was writing *Following the Color Line* and John Daniels started his survey of Boston when I started my survey of New York. A thrilling subject, the American Negro; some worthwhile people to be found championing his rights, the kindest consideration from the Negroes themselves.

So I gathered information and each month knew a little more of my subject.

1 October 1932

Two Leaders

Many of the younger generation today think of Washington as a myth and of Du Bois as a back number. But at the time that I began my investigations these two men filled the stage, overshadowing other figures. And, with due respect to the youth of the present time, they were greater figures than the new generation has yet produced.

Of Washington I can only speak as a casual acquaintance. He was far too busy a man to give his time to a woman of very moderate means who, if she subscribed at all to his school, would not be able to go beyond the ten dollar bill. He meant Tuskegee to be one of the best-equipped, best-taught schools in America. Such time as he could take from his work, his home, and his friends was needed in making contacts that would bring him large returns.

I first met him through John E. Milholland at the Hotel Manhattan, where he always stayed. He gave me one of the best pieces of advice I have ever had: "Always ask for more money than you think you can get. I made the mistake of asking Carnegie for six hundred thousand. I believe he would have given me a million."

Mr. Washington's autobiography, *Up from Slavery,* is still one of the world's best-sellers. The story of how he dusted the schoolroom at Hampton three times over and was accepted because of his thoroughness is typical of his zest for perfection, his ability to eat up work. He had a great flow of ideas, and, when at Tuskegee (much of his time was taken up with raising money), he kept his teachers so long in consultation that they had to neglect their classes. When he boarded a train the faculty drew a sigh of relief, but soon telegrams came ordering innovations. He introduced many of the best methods of today for rural education.

Farm demonstration work was done by Tuskegee long before the government took it up. From Hampton he learned the value of relating education to life, and it became a religion with him. His people were struggling, often blindly, for a chance to develop their power. He told them to do this where they were, to become master workmen.

His famous Atlanta speech, "put down your buckets where you are," applied to the colored laborer as well as to the white employer. Hard work was now divorced from slavery. The Negro must respect it, must buy land, plant crops, whitewash houses, clean up back-yards.

One time he sent word to the Negroes for miles around Tuskegee to come to the school. They obeyed. When they got there he told them to go back and clean up their yards.

His favorite animal was the pig because, as he says in "Working with the Hands," it brings in the largest returns.

Many of his graduates went out to teach, and the gospel of making the most of life where you are spread among the race.

Of course, the whites ate up this doctrine. Some distrusted him in the South; he spent too much time in the North, where social equality was practiced, but the North found him a glorious prophet. The Negro had of late been a harassing responsibility. Now someone had come with a happy solution of the whole problem. Cease to think of lynchings, of injustice, of the loss of the ballot. Help the Negro to help himself. Make the Negro a good workman by giving money to Tuskegee. Washington was greeted with acclaim and with profound relief. He lectured in the largest hall the town he visited could offer and saw many turned away. Large gifts of money came to him and Tuskegee grew.

From the beginning there was an element among the Negroes that viewed the situation with alarm. Monroe Trotter of Boston was the first to offer resistance and landed in jail.

Jealousy of Washington's power grew. He held the purse strings. Whom he endorsed received dollars for their enterprises, while those he failed to endorse had to be contented with stray pennies.

The whites wrote to him about everything—the number of bath tubs for the YMCA (did the Negro really care to wash?), the best book on the color question. Washington was too level-headed to become an Emperor Jones, but he enjoyed his power and meant to keep it. He was surrounded with followers, not equals. A stream of young teachers entered Tuskegee one year and a swift-running rill left it the next. Some felt the place too much a spectacle. They could no longer endure the procession entering the chapel to the blare of trumpets, with the white visitor infallibly rising to exclaim with the Queen of Sheba, "The half was not told me." Others found the principal failed to uphold their authority with their pupils. And outside the school, from Monroe Trotter on, men began to question Washington's leadership.

The white world, in the meantime, was delighted with their panacea. "Give money to Hampton and Tuskegee," they said, "teach the Negro to be a good worker, and other needful things will be added."

But when Washington rose to power, other things were taken away.

To vote in the South became impossible.

School funds were voted by the legislature according to the per capita population, and divided by the whites among themselves. This gave the southern portion of a state like Alabama an enormous advantage over the northern part, where there were no Negro children to be counted out.

Public opinion, moreover, demanded that the Negroes should not complain. They must work hard and live in friendly relations with their white neighbors. In the cities Negro quarters were unimproved, high schools did not exist and should not be demanded. Industrial education was enough. This affected the schools supported by philanthropy.

Even Fisk University had to introduce industrial training. And Washington said nothing against this. He probably felt that it was his job to look after his school. Let others look out for themselves.

I used to be amused and saddened by what I saw. Before long I was known as one interested in the Negro and I had many calls from colored men and women who needed money for their work. Almost invariably, they began by handing me some recommendation from Washington endorsing them. It might be a note or perhaps only a newspaper clipping. It was presented as more precious than gold. I would say casually: "But I am not in sympathy with Dr. Washington's opinion. Industrial training is only a small part of what the Negro needs."

Then it was as though an actor dropped his mask. One man said to me with tears in his eyes: "I've sat on Washington's doorstep for four years to get this piece of paper. I couldn't raise a penny without it. Four years."

When the mask was dropped, I would have a real talk, a talk as between equals, and I would learn that every Negro worth his salt wanted the same thing, his rights as a citizen of this republic.

There was one school that Washington never captured. Atlanta University. Here that good old New Englander, Horace Bumstead, was president, and here instruction in higher education went on without apology. And here was the only Negro who at any time was a serious rival to Washington, Burghardt Du Bois.

Dr. Du Bois has written a slight sketch of his life in *Dark Water.* He had no dramatic background of dire poverty. He was poor, but so were the most of his public school playmates, the farmers' and factory workers' boys and girls. He grew up in the Berkshires and had a higher education than his classmates, taking his Ph.D. at Harvard after graduate study at the University of Berlin. He wrote a monumental volume on the Negro in Philadelphia and then went to Atlanta, where he remained for many years heading the department of economics and instituting the Atlanta Sociological Studies, the first extensive sociological studies of Negro conditions in the United States.

I made his acquaintance originally through his writing. Some of the essays in *The Souls of Black Folk* appeared first in the *Atlantic Monthly*, where I saw them and learned of the inhumanity of race prejudice. I wrote to him as soon as I received my fellowship, asking his advice. He was unendingly kind. I have a file of his letters with me now in which he advises me regarding my method of attack, gives me introductions to important men and women, accepts some of my criticisms of his writing. I seem to have been free with criticism and, in return, gave criticism.

At the end of a year, knowing that his studies required support, at some sacrifice, I sent a check for twenty dollars to the University's Sociological Fund. In his letter of thanks he expressed disappointment: "I didn't know," he said, "that I was dealing with a mere millionaire." Back of the joke was something real. Du Bois and his followers wanted from the white man something more than money. They wanted a state of mind.

I attended two notable conferences in 1906, reporting each for the New York *Evening Post*, of which Oswald Garrison Villard was then the editor. One was the Niagara Movement, headed by Du Bois, the other the National Negro Business League, headed by Washington.

The league was an effort of Washington to get the Negroes who were accomplishing something in business to meet and pool their experiences that they might learn from one another. It met in the summer in Atlanta shortly before the terrible riots. The sessions were designed to be practical talks, though oratory occasionally added savor to the feast. There were, I remember, a few contractors. One from New Orleans did a large business, a number of bankers, and some men in real estate.

Philip Payton of New York was in the audience. I went down the church aisle and talked with him, but, though we were in a colored church, I could see that I made him uneasy. Lynchings were going on at that time in the city and perhaps he was right in thinking that my cordial greeting might endanger him. It was the farmers, however, who gave the meetings color and interest. They told noble tales of money made in cotton and corn.

"And don't let your neighbor know you got a cent," one advised. "Money's harder ter keep than ter make."

Through all the meetings, Washington presided with great tact. When the talk grew acrimonious, he came in with an amusing story. Everyone paid him tribute. He had succeeded, and they, working hard under great difficulties, looked up to him to show them success. There was no good in cursing the white man. He was on the scene to stay. Rather, they should take advantage of race prejudice and so improve their businesses that Negroes would support them.

A little before the Negro League came the Niagara Movement meeting at Harpers Ferry, where John Brown made his stand for freedom. It was attended by about one hundred men and women of the "Intelligentsia." They were from different parts of the country, the North largely predominating. Storer College housed us, and between the meetings, which were not burdensome, there was opportunity for long discussions and good times. I was very diligent, as this was my first newspaper assignment, and I wanted to do my best. But I met the members at meal times and in the evening when my work was done, and managed to have more than one discussion, or rather conversation, for I was wholeheartedly in accord with the platform of these insurgents.

The John Brown fort, now on the grounds of Storer College, was then in a field at a distance, and we made a pilgrimage there early one morning. I can see Dr. Owen M. Waller walking barefooted through the rough grass and stones to the shrine of this old warrior, who with a handful of supporters stood against the millions of the slaveholding South. There was one young man who would have looked handsomer in a movie than any favorite we have today. He said he had the blood of the Randolphs in his veins. I don't doubt it. I only doubt whether any Randolph was as aristocratic as he.

There was Frederick McGhee, big, black, respected by all his community, a representative of Minnesota. There were a number of women, some of them of great beauty. The work of the year was retailed—a few cases of discrimination carried up to higher courts. Even one as inexperienced as I saw that legal work could not possibly be carried on by the Movement's small fees. But there was purpose and enthusiasm. We sang "John Brown's Body" at the end of every meeting, and we sang as though inspired.

In one way we were more conservative than Booker Washington. We had our meals regularly and on time. In Atlanta I had taken notes until four in the afternoon, and then found the second meeting coming at once upon the end of the first. The Negro stores up food as the camel stores up water. We anemic whites are not so stoic. We like a luncheon.

In the Address to the Country which the Niagara Movement gave the press, five things were demanded: the vote, the abolition of jim-crowing, equal enforcement of the law, education on the same basis as education for the white, "The right to associate with such people as wish to associate with us." It was written by Du Bois and magnificently read by Mr. L. M. Hershaw of Washington. It could appropriately be read today.

Among the distinguished visitors to the Business League and the Niagara Movement was Richard T. Greener, the first colored man to graduate from Harvard College. Greener had lately returned from Vladivostock, where he had been United States consul. He made an address at each place. At Harpers Ferry he spoke of the battle for freedom. He eulogized John Brown and consecrated his race anew to the struggle for human rights. His speech ended with the words, "Who would be free himself must strike the blow."

Later, at the Business League, he talked of compromise, of the necessity of adjusting one's self to circumstance, ending with the quotation, "It is better to bend than to break."

He left the platform after his speech and walked down the aisle and saw me taking notes. We had met and talked together at

Harpers Ferry. There was embarrassment in his manner as he nodded and hurried past.

Both of his pieces of advice held a good deal of truth, and an old man might be permitted to utter them both with conviction. He had done his work and was past the time for taking sides. But the leaders and many of their followers were young and could not believe that both sides were right. Fortunately for the race, they were able to choose where they should stand. Solidarity is good, but independence of thought is better. Where the Negro suffered and still suffers is in his inability to express his aspirations. Following Washington's advice, he paints his house and then is thrown out of it because it looks better than the house of his white neighbor. How shall he ever have the right to live in it, save as his aspirations seem to his race to be worth battle and sacrifice?

8 October 1932

Living on San Juan Hill

Not living on San Juan Hill in Cuba up which the colored soldiers charged, but on San Juan Hill in New York, a poor neighborhood running from West 60th Street, to West 64th Street, between 10th and 11th Avenues. Whites dwelt on the avenues, colored on the streets, and fights between the two gave the hill its name. A rough neighborhood, but, at least among the Negroes, a place where all classes lived.

There were people who itched for a fight, and people who hated roughness. Lewd women leaned out of windows, and neat, hard-working mothers early each morning made their way to their mistresses' homes. Men lounged on street corners in as dandified dress as their women at the wash tubs could get for them; while hardworking porters and longshoremen, night watchmen and government clerks, went regularly to their jobs. Race prejudice and economic necessity threw all sorts and conditions of colored people together. I speak of the San Juan Hill of the past. I know little about it now, but when in January 1908, I moved into the Tuskegee Apartments, built by Henry Phipps, its reputation was little better than Hell's Kitchen, the picturesque Irish gangster neighborhood a few blocks south.

John E. Milholland, whose name should be revered by all of us, was instrumental in having the Tuskegee Apartments built. He knew that Henry Phipps was building model tenements, to return four percent on the investment. Milholland, learning through me of the frightful housing conditions among the Negro working class, persuaded Phipps to put his second venture in a Negro neighborhood. So, the Hill saw a fireproof, new-law tenement, with steam heat and unlimited hot water, in the midst of its double-decker and dumbbell apartments that covered ninety percent of each building lot. The management was in the hands of the City and Suburban Homes Company.

I had begun my settlement work in a model tenement erected by Charles Pratt. My next venture was in a tenement erected by Henry Phipps, and, while Mr. Phipps had as yet shown no interest in settlement work, caring only for the housing end, I hoped by quietly renting on my own account, to persuade him to add social service work.

The house had a playroom for its children, which the Walton Free Kindergarten was allowed to occupy in the morning. I could develop more work that later might be supported. So, I took a little furniture, a great many books, and moved into my flat. It had three rooms and a bath.

Life among working-class people was familiar to me, but I found that San Juan Hill was very different from Greenpoint. There was, of course, the difference of race, or color, but I soon forgot that. The noticeable difference was in the lower economic status of the Negro.

Greenpoint had been a factory neighborhood, and, though the work had been hard, it had been fairly constant. Girls worked in factories and shops; men worked regularly at skilled and unskilled labor. All got a decent wage, so that the housewife stayed at home, giving her full time to her family's wants. On San Juan Hill this was the exception, not the rule.

There were families where the husband and older children supported the household, but, usually, the mother had to help support the family. She did this by taking in laundry, or she went out to service. As a domestic, she would be away for twelve or fourteen hours. If she went out to clean, she put in eight hours of work. When she got home she must at once attend to her husband and children. Her babies were boarded with some old and inefficient woman, unless she was lucky enough to get them in the nursery. When they grew older they lived in the street. That was safer than leaving them locked in at home.

The men were unskilled laborers, some longshoremen, a decently paid group, some porters in factory or store. Some were general utility men in boarding-houses, with hours as long as the women's. Many a boarding-house employs such a man, who works early and late about the place, receiving a scant wage. Men worked at night as watchmen, and must sleep through the day's noise. And, lastly, far more than at Greenpoint, men did not work at all, either because they could not get jobs or because the jobs they might secure were hateful, and they could find some woman—wife, mother, or sweetheart—to support them. These men lounged on street corners during the day or played pool in one of the many pool rooms.

The absence of the mother from the home led to juvenile delinquency. More than white children, colored boys and girls came before the juvenile court for improper guardianship. That was the only offense where the Negro percentage was higher than the white. I know, for I spent many late afternoons going over the juvenile court records in the stuffy courthouse. Ruth Draper, then a young girl, a member of the Junior League and working at Greenwich House, used to help me. I wish she might have seen the cases instead of the records only. We went patiently over the pages and learned that environment was the determining factor in juvenile arrests. Where, as in a Jewish neighborhood, the pushcart stood temptingly by the sidewalk, there petty larceny abounded. And where, as on San Juan Hill, mothers had to go out to work, arrests were numerous for improper guardianship. Our researches exploded the loose accusation that Negroes are born with a propensity to steal. The colored child stole no more and no less than the average white child.

My best friend on San Juan Hill was the Rev. George Simms of the Union Baptist Church. Since San Juan Hill has become a West Indian neighborhood, his church has moved to Harlem, but, when I knew it, it was frequented chiefly by newly arrived Southerners. They went to the Union Baptist Church and found themselves at home, got "happy," and were not frowned upon, though they never got beyond their minister's control.

His sermons were madly picturesque and yet full of common sense. He could preach as vivid a sermon as any in *God's Trombones*. His picture of Jesus in his blue smock leaving his carpenter's bench to be baptized by John the Baptist belongs in *The Green Pastures*.

He cooperated with all of us on the Hill, the kindergartners, the day nursery workers, the superintendent of the Tuskegee. The suffragists came to his church, and he made the best speech of any. He had a rival in one of his deacons, known as Brother Baptist.

Once, when an anti-suffragist complained that, if women were given the vote, the women who walked the streets would be enfranchised, Brother Baptist said in answer: "Yes, we knows dey's women

walkin' de streets. Dey's walkin' de streets right now. But who's
walking wid 'em?"

Eight months was not a long time to study a neighborhood, and
I had my book to write as well as committees to attend, but I managed to see a good deal. With a tenement house inspector, for ten
days I climbed thousands of stairs. The white homes we looked into,
homes bordering on the Negro neighborhood, were more dirty than
the colored. They seemed to contain a great many mangy dogs. But
the Negro, however poor, did not surrender the attempt to make her
home attractive. A white spread or a calico quilt would be on the bed,
the china on the shelf would be gay and neatly arranged, the room
usually fairly clean. The standard may have come from intimate
acquaintance with the homes of well-to-do mistresses, but it was
there. The streets, too, though they knew fighting and heard guffaws
of laughter and screams of terror, preserved a certain decency. I can
illustrate this in no better way than by the fact that I never saw the
obscene writing that had been common in Greenpoint.

I thought of this one day when I was poking about in an inner
court to find the home of an impoverished child. The walls offered
space for the gross offers I had grown familiar with years before. But
instead, on one of these walls, in a neat handwriting, I read: "Unless
above himself he can erect himself, how poor a thing is man." And
below: "No conflict is so severe as his who labors to subdue himself.
But in this we must continually be engaged if we would strengthen
the inner man."

I would not imply that it was usual to find Shakespeare and
Thomas à Kempis written upon the walls. I never saw them again.
But the imagination and religious fervor that they expressed were
familiar to these sordid city blocks.

Negro children, when taught good manners, enjoyed practicing them. Some of the children on my street were a delight to entertain. I loved to have them come to my flat, their hair standing out in
two little braids, their eyes bright, their hands slender and pretty. If
one handed me a flower, it was done with grace.

I remember walking down my block with an old Greenpoint
friend and seeing a boy of eight run up to his mother, kiss her, and
then take a parcel from her arms. "That's not unusual," I said to my
friend. Quick as a flash, her Irish wit responded: "Then you needn't
be explaining to me the reason for the high death rate among
children."

The darkest part of life on the Hill was the realization that so little was ahead for these same children. Poverty was their lot. I remember Annabel, who came running to me one evening to say that her mother would the next day be turned out into the street. She had supported the family by laundry work until sickness came and now the threatened dispossession. I went to her apartment.

"It is the end," she said, offering me the one chair left. That morning she had sold the furniture and on the way home lost the money. "It is the end." Organized charity came the next day and paid the rent, but there followed a long period of want and suffering. Annabel told me one day what she expected to do when she grew up. "I shall dance," she declared. "Dancers make money. I shall not work the way my mother does. She works and works and never has anything."

At the end of eight months I saw that my settlement dream would never be realized. Mr. Phipps was interested in housing, but his interest stopped there. In the one interview I had with him, I could not convince him of the value of all that I hoped to do. The City and Suburban Homes Company also took no interest in supporting my plans.

I suspect they thought a settlement in a model tenement would be a nuisance. I saw my savings rapidly disappearing and no chance of a salary. So, when the summer was over, very reluctantly I gave up my apartment and for a second time left busy, warm-hearted working-class neighbors for middle-class respectability. It would have been harder to do this had I not been greatly needed at home.

In all the months that I lived, a white woman alone in a block with five thousand Negroes, I never had a disagreeable experience. I was never accosted rudely. The race riots of which I had heard had ceased to occur. Some of my friends thought I was running a risk. One called me up after dining with me and, in forceful language in which the word "Nigger" was present, told me I should leave. I told him I was as safe there as anywhere. Danger is never absent, but I did not taste it.

The colored people, more than the whites in Greenpoint, took me for exactly what I was. Had they been better educated, more sophisticated, they might have been suspicious of my sincerity. But I was among big-hearted, friendly, hard-working human beings. They thought me a teacher and put me down at that.

It spoke well for the work that had gone before mine, public

school, mission, kindergarten, health department, charity organization society—that I was understood. They saw that I wanted to help.
They believed that I respected them in their terrific struggle to make
life easier for their children.

It was many months before I mastered my disappointment and
years before I ceased to think of that street and my home on it. I had
met the Negro race and felt its charm, that charm that New York has
not yet wholly destroyed.

In the evening at my open window on the crowded street I
hear the children calling to one another in their play. They have a
street song, "Sound dem weddin' bells," that I have not heard before.
. . . An evangelist moves past me, saying, "Salvation is so convenient,
don't forget that. Friends, it's convenient. It's for this world." . . . An
old woman, in a high, shaking voice sings, "Give me Jesus, give me
Jesus. You may have all this world but give me Jesus." . . . It is afternoon. A knock comes at my door. I open it, and three little girls, in
freshly laundered white dresses, slip shyly in. The oldest, she has
lived five whole years, opens her hand and offers me one of two
peanuts. I tell them about Peter Rabbit, and their eyes are bright like
Peter's. And their little dark hands, lying on their white dresses, are
so expressive, so delicately moulded, that I forget about Peter Rabbit
and everything else as I look at them.

15 October 1932

That Cosmopolitan Club Dinner: I Meet the Reporters

$\mathcal{I}$ have spoken of the Cosmopolitan Club, an organization made up of white and colored men and women for the discussion of present day problems. While it was small, numbering about thirty members, for a moment it achieved fame. Its doings were reported North and South and East and West. Especially did it reverberate in the South. It gave a dinner.

In 1908 New York was becoming a restaurant city. The boarding-house was giving way to the lodging-house and countless people were going out to their meals. A restaurant would rent one of its rooms to an organization for the evening, thus giving the diner a free hall in which he could hold a meeting and talk of anything he chose. One of the favorite New York places at that time for groups with more ideas than money was Peck's restaurant on lower Fulton Street. This the Cosmopolitan Club secured for a given night and proceeded to sell tickets.

The tickets went well, for the speakers advertised were prominent men. Among the whites were Oswald Garrison Villard, of the *Evening Post;* Hamilton Holt, of the *Independent;* John Spargo, brilliant speaker for the Socialist party. Among the Negro speakers were William H. Ferris, later one of Garvey's foremost workers, and the Rev. George Frazier Miller. Dr. Owen M. Waller presided.

The colored people who went to the dinner for the most part were the old-fashioned group, living in Brooklyn, that I have attempted to describe. A few were Socialists, but the majority believed that the best thing that had ever been said regarding the rights of individuals was said by Jefferson in the opening to the Declaration of Independence. They would be satisfied if they could get as good a chance in America as the white man. The whites were of various ideas, people like Villard of old-time abolition heritage, Socialists, radicals, social workers, friends of members of the club. I doubt if there was more than one person there under thirty. It was a sober gathering.

We had singularly good speeches. Kennedy's "Servant in the House" was being acted, and more than one referred to the Christ who figured as the servant. With the exception of Spargo's and Miller's Socialist appeals, no panacea was offered. Holt was the only person to mention miscegenation and then to dismiss it. The beauty of human brotherhood, the thought that all men can work together for good, was the dominant word. I have never heard Oswald Garrison Villard make a more moving spiritual appeal. As we went out, we said to one another that it had been good to be there.

Now while this was the spirit of the meeting and of the club, a few members were up to mischief. The president of the Cosmopolitan Club was Andre Tridon, a Frenchman and delightful pagan. He and one or two others had invited reporters. When they appeared and wanted to take a flashlight picture, Mr. Villard told me that trouble was ahead. I refused to allow the picture to be taken and then forgot about the reporters. They were recalled to me the next morning!

The story went over the country. Negro and white had sat down together in a restaurant in New York and talked miscegenation. No speech was given any space except the few remarks that Holt made when he gave the four possible solutions of the race problem, one of them miscegenation. But the speeches were not the real news. The news was the dinner itself and the reporters had industriously gathered the names of the guests, especially of the women. By the time the story got thoroughly drenched in their imagination, the gathering became a meeting of voluptuous white women and smirking Negro men. As all the newspaper writers were men, there was no remark made of the presence of Negro women by white men. The white men were called fools, but the white women were rated lower than that.

Editors throughout the country gave their opinions.

"We have bitter contempt," the Richmond *Leader* said, "for the whites that participated in it and illustrated that degeneracy will seek its level."

"This miscegenation dinner was loathsome enough to consign the whole fraternity of perverts who participated in it to undying infamy," said the St. Louis *Dispatch*.

Burleson of Texas said that the affair was "unbelievable, abhorrent, and inconceivable."

Tillman raised the bloody shirt, declaring: "This incident, trivial in itself, only marks the rapid progress we are making toward the inevitable catastrophe. I have contended for years that existing conditions can have but one end, bloody conflicts."

The longest and most picturesque account was by Judge Thomas N. Norwood in the Savannah *News*. Sometimes the judge was funny. He told of the two Desdemonas, on either side an Othello, who told his exploits in the Spanish-American War. Mrs. Sterling, a woman then about seventy, was described leaning amorously against a very black West Indian. Young girls (one young Western girl was present with her mother) dressed in décolleté, dropped their heads on black men's shoulders. Worst of all, was

> the high priestess, Miss Ovington, whose father is rich and who affiliates five days in every week with Negro men and dines with them at her home in Brooklyn on Sunday. She could have had a hundred thousand Negroes at the Bacchanal feast had she waved the bread tray. But the horror of it is she could take young white girls into that den. This is the feature that should alarm and arouse Northern society.
>
> But our horror over the decadent women is only equalled by our amazement to see editors of papers that hitherto have been considered decent, and a reputable writer for magazines, in that witches' cauldron on that black night.

Thus spoke our enemies. We who were present said little. I saw more reporters the week after the event than I had seen before in my whole life, but I could only give my mild version of the affair. The *Evening Post* carried a letter or two and the *Independent* a short editorial. There were a few days of hubbub and the dinner's news value was over.

My name and address were in the paper. I had been one of the speakers, and I came in for the most publicity. My mail was very heavy.

My address had been given at the Hotel St. George, Brooklyn, where I went from the Phipps tenement for my weekend. As I entered the foyer, I felt conspicuous. I remember the mail clerk, Taylor, a colored man, and how considerate he was when I approached the desk. He had my mail in his hand that I might not be obliged to stay in the lobby an extra moment. He said nothing, but I felt his sympathy. The mail was of all sorts. A few friendly letters, congratulating me, letters from Negroes regretting what I was going through, and the rest showing contempt or scorn. Some were threatening. That was rather jolly. One is complimented to feel that one may have endangered one's life for a cause. Some were very severe but dignified. The bulk were illiterate and nauseatingly obscene. I was smothered in mud. Like so many of the women of my class, I had led a sheltered life. That mail, entirely from the South, taught me much. It did not endear me to that section! When I read of a lynching today, I think of those letters and know the men who engineered it.

I had one letter from the South that I loved. It came from a man in a little town of Maryland. It was written in a scraggly hand and was only a few lines. "I am a white man," it said, "but I glory in your spunk in standing up for what you believe to be right."

Among all the newspaper editorials, I am inclined to think the Louisville *Courier-Journal* made the sanest remark. The reporter for the *New York Times* had written that he had not seen any "story." The *Courier-Journal* said of the story:

> It is not altogether improbable that the reporter for the "yellow" journal was guilty of more or less exaggeration, but according to the canon of journalism there was material for a story. The definition of news that obtains in every city room includes the unusual. It is unusual for white and colored people to dine together in North America. It is futile for the defenders of the mixing-of-the-races-dinner to quarrel with a reporter for taking notice of the unusualness of the event.

Looking back on it now, this comment seems to me correct. It was unusual for white and colored to dine together in public in New York, and, since the reporters were invited to see this, they made the most of the occurrence.

But the dinner accomplished one important thing. The dining of white and colored together in New York ceased to be news.

The next year a smaller but similar dinner took place, and the papers did not notice it. Of recent years dinners have been given by so many organizations, to so many distinguished colored people, at which the races have been about equal in number, that no reporter would bother to mention that black and white sat down together.

We at the Cosmopolitan Club were pioneers. We suffered the notoriety of pioneers, but we did a good piece of work. In 1931 a committee of prominent New Yorkers gave a dinner to James Weldon Johnson at the Hotel Pennsylvania. I sat next to Carl Van Doren, and, as he looked at the list of the dinner committee, he said, "This is the most distinguished list of names I have ever seen on a dinner invitation." I studied the people at the tables, white and colored side by side, and felt as though I were turning the pages of *Who's Who,* finding not only writers and artists but men of affairs.

Mr. Villard came over to speak to me between two courses.

"You and I can't be discouraged on this race question," he said. "The world does move. Think of the Cosmopolitan Club dinner."

22 October 1932

I Go South

The Southerner likes to tell the Northerner who studies the Negro question that he was not born in the South.

Well, I couldn't change that, but I could go South and try to learn what made that land so different that the whites clung to chattel slavery after the rest of the world had repudiated it. I knew the reason given by the Southern slaveholder: that the Negro was of an inferior race, incapable of higher education, working only under compulsion. This made the slave block possible. I would study conditions then south of the Mason and Dixon line.

My first trip, no farther than Hampton, was particularly unfortunate if I were to see the low mentality of the black race. I was invited to a summer conference, where educated people met and discussed their problems. This was my first large Negro gathering, before the Niagara Movement and the Business League, of which I have written. I was surprised, great as my expectations had been, at the clarity of thought and ability of statement of the men and women gathered there. In every debate the points made were those one wanted made.

These Negroes could have debated any Southern writer I had read and wiped the floor with him. Thomas Nelson Page, Thomas Dixon, Smith of Tulane, would have grown angry, but they would not have brought conviction to an unprejudiced listener.

Moton was there, a young man of powerful physique, mobile face, and immaculate white uniform. It takes the cheap labor of an industrial school to keep one in white clothes. Sarah Forten Grimké was present, reminding me of my mother's mother, the same clear mind and the same expressive hands. Hands mean more to me than faces.

Everyone was kind and ready to answer my questions, though at times they must have been bored. It was lovely June weather and

37

Hampton was at its best. Dr. Frissell's welcome was then, as always, cordial, for I made the school many visits.

The next year Atlanta University called me South to its sociological conference. Despite the ugly buildings and the seedy-looking campus, I found it perfect, for here white and colored met on a complete equality and one became unconscious of race. How I did enjoy that Atlanta visit with dear old Dr. Crogman at Clark, Dr. Hope at Morehouse, with the Townes and Herndons and other houses open to me and with Dr. and Mrs. Du Bois at the university welcoming me whenever I wanted to drop in at their rooms. If they were not at home, I enjoyed their wonderful library. Supper at Atlanta in the old dining room, teachers and students together (good food that was meant for the students), with singing afterwards was unforgettable.

This was the spring before the Atlanta riots and ugly stories were in the air. Negroes were lynched for the most trivial happenings. Max Barber was editing *The Voice of the Negro,* and he and I did a foolhardy thing, riding together in an open carriage through Atlanta's streets. People stared hard, for by no possibility could he pass for white or I for colored. But we arrived safely at Mrs. Hunton's home, where Eunice and Alpheus, little tots then, entertained us while their mother prepared supper.

My first lengthy visit to the South was in the winter of 1906–1907. Mr. Milholland had seen a letter of mine on the Atlanta courts in the New York *Evening Post* and had liked it so much that he offered to pay my expenses if I would go again and write more of the same kind. I didn't dare accept his proposition. I was afraid I couldn't write as well as that again, but I accepted some financial aid and went back to Atlanta for a week and then to Calhoun, Alabama.

Calhoun Colored School, founded by Charlotte R. Thorn and Mabel Dillingham, is among the most picturesque schools of the South. It is in the black belt, twenty-odd miles south of Montgomery. These two women were young teachers at Hampton when Booker Washington, returning to visit the school in which he was trained, urged the need of more schools farther South. They asked him to name a place where they should go. He wrote later recommending Calhoun. "The Negroes have been praying for a school there," he said, "so I guess they want it." The two women, quite literally, went in answer to prayer. The white people were hostile. Food had to be hidden lest it be poisoned; students' lives were threatened. Miss Dillingham soon died from hardship, but Miss Thorn lived to be over seventy and her school continues.

The monotony of red clay and dark pines, of shabby little houses devoid of paint, did not reassure me as I left the train at Calhoun and was driven in a quaint open carriage to my destination. But at the campus I found New England. Neat white buildings with green blinds. Miss Thorn's cottage, covered with rose vines, flower-bordered walks, order, cleanliness, beauty, all these were present, in striking contrast to the countryside through which my train had passed. I went in to supper and at the principal's table met some of the teachers, white and colored.

The next day, Sunday, I attended afternoon service and heard spirituals sung as I had never heard them before and was never to hear them again. (Except once at Hampton in the days when Moton led.) Sitting on the platform and looking at the earnest faces, I knew that it was fear, not contempt, that had kept the slaveholders and, after the war, the planters from giving education to these people. They knew the Negro's capability, but they had not learned what we have all been so slow in learning, that an educated working class produces more for the community than a slave one.

Charlotte R. Thorn died in September 1932. For years she had suffered from attacks of severe illness, but her spirit surmounted them and brought recovery. At length, with old age, that spirit could no longer control the body. I saw her when she was in her prime, when the plans that she had for her school were being rapidly carried out and she was her happiest. She brought to the people her culture, her gay spirits, her belief in the immense possibilities of all peoples. She believed that the Negro child, like any other normal child, would respond to the standard set up for it.

As an example: Ray Stannard Baker was writing *Following the Color Line* that winter and stopped for a night at Calhoun. I was with Miss Thorn when he asked her a series of questions, among them one regarding the honesty of the boys and girls. He prefaced his remarks by saying that he knew the Negro stole but that he realized the habit came from slavery.

Miss Thorn said in reply: "Yes, we have had stealing." She stopped to recall the facts exactly. "We have had two cases since I came here fifteen years ago. One was the theft of an old dress that was in a teacher's room. This, however, was not by a pupil but by a woman of the community. The other was the theft of a hair ribbon by one of our own girls. She was told that she must leave her dormitory and live in the community until we could trust her again. Later she came back to us."

I can see Mr. Baker's face now when this extraordinary record of honesty was given him, better than anything he could have quoted from a white school. But in Montgomery, where he had recently stopped, it was true that the poorly paid Negro servant of whom little was expected stole food and clothing from her mistress.

Christmas that year was very cold and the boys were busy keeping up the fires. Miss Thorn's fireplace was piled high with logs. Another of her guests was Leslie Pinckney Hill, then a teacher at Tuskegee. I remember how we two walked briskly round and round the little campus and longed for a good run over the hills. We were like refugees sheltered in a consulate during a war, in danger of lynching if we went outside together. The day was full of celebrations and the students' dinner was glorious to see and smell. Our celebration ended with a good time in the modest assembly hall.

In the morning some of the boys had taken baskets to the poor in the community. As Miss Thorn and I were coming out of the hall, the day's celebrations over, we met a boy of about seventeen. Miss Thorn stopped and wanted to know why he had been away so long. He explained that the woman with whom he was to leave a Christmas basket had moved and it had taken all day to reach her home and return. He said he was glad he had found the old woman and that she seemed right pleased. Then, with a good-night, he left us. I was impressed not only by his unselfishness, he had missed the turkey dinner and all the good times, but also by his not dramatizing the event. He had been sent out to do a job and he had done it. That was all. Back of such a personality is power.

That was what impressed me more than anything else at Calhoun, earnestness and latent power. Under different direction our Negro peasantry could have grown up in the South as the European peasantry developed.

Calhoun owned some hundreds of acres, which it sold to the thrifty element in the community. Those Negroes who were not on the school's land worked for the most part for a single landlord, a man hated by all his tenants, white and black. He had been known to drive his men to work at the point of a pistol. He did not dare beat the whites as he did the Negroes, but he managed to keep them in his debt. At election time, however, they became men of a superior race. Race pride sustained them in their poverty.

One day Miss Thorn, her nephew, Sidney Dickerson (now a distinguished artist), and I took the train to Montgomery. We occupied two seats in the day coach facing one another. A white woman from Calhoun got on the same train and sat opposite us. She was dirty, poorly dressed, with frowsy hair and a small, tight mouth. When she saw Miss Thorn she turned her back on her. It was an uncomfortable position, but she maintained it for the hour's ride. Miss Thorn's eyes danced and an amused smile was on Sidney Dickerson's face. The whites were not forgotten at Calhoun, and they accepted anything offered them or their children. But Miss Thorn taught "niggers" and should be insulted in public. In turning her back on this teacher, however, the woman turned her back on the march of civilization. The Negro in the school faced it, ran toward it, and outstripped her and her kind.

29 October 1932

The Far South

One of the persons whom Mr. Milholland wanted me to meet was Joseph Manning, Republican office holder, appointed postmaster at Alexander City, Alabama, in the center of the state. Mr. Manning used to call himself a "hillbilly." He had been a Populist in his early days and had a natural sympathy for the underdog. Because he wrote favorably of the Negro in a paper he was printing with Mr. Milholland's assistance, he had been attacked and beaten up by two of the most ruffianly looking men I have ever seen. (I saw them at the Methodist church.) Manning was married and had six children. He paid a woman a small percentage of his salary to run the post office. I never saw him do any work. He was delighted to meet a person with congenial views and told me his troubles and the condition of the Negroes in the city. His wife, his superior socially, was a hard-working, quiet woman, who perhaps out of courtesy, expressed sympathy for the black man. The oldest son, a boy of eleven, had great promise, but he was already burdened with home cares.

This was my first visit in a white home in the South since I had begun my investigations. I followed Mr. Manning's instructions and for the first week saw only the white world. I spoke in the Methodist church, whose minister was an able, kindly man. I met a few of Manning's friends, and I visited the white schools. The largest school was directly opposite the Manning home.

Dilatoriness, I saw, was not confined to colored people. The Manning children were never once, while I was there, on time for school. The teacher confided to me that she could never start at nine. One night the Methodist minister had supper with us, and, as I was to speak on settlement work at his church at seven, I watched the clock. But he ignored it and we did not get to the church until half past seven. Even then we were too soon. Colored People's Time is evidently derived from Southern People's Time.

I had a queer feeling that week. I knew that I was out of agreement with the white world in which I was mingling, and I knew that the white people knew it. The Methodist minister liked me and wanted his wife to entertain me. Three times I was invited to his home for a meal, and three times the invitation was withdrawn at the last minute. I never saw the minister's wife. She knew that I was a "nigger lover," as the South gracefully puts it, and she did not mean that I should darken her home. In the evening some friend of Mr. Manning's might drop in and we would talk on economic problems when I was not receiving information regarding conditions in Alexander City. The men seemed interested in the outside world.

At the end of the week I turned to the colored world. The Methodist minister went with me when I visited the Negro school. Of course, the principal called all the classes together and asked us to address them. What platitudes those poor Southern children have to listen to! When anyone comes to visit they are called from their work to listen to some "dear children" talk. Mr. Manning had a story of a white teacher who came North and visited the principal of a famous school in Springfield, Massachusetts. "I shall be glad to speak to every class," the Southerner said. Well, the minister and Manning and I all spoke. I told the children what fun the Northern boys and girls were having at home coasting on their sleds. I made them quite envious. The other two spoke to them as "good children." The next night Manning and I spoke at a colored church, where for the first time I felt at home.

William Benson, of Kowaliga, had driven in to hear us and to take us the next day to his school. We had a carriage to ourselves, since it would not have been safe for us to have driven with him. We visited his school and saw the remarkable community work that this young Negro was doing. He is dead now and his experiment forgotten, but he was one of the farsighted men of his race, too farsighted to receive adequate support. He took a community and tried to meet, not only its educational, but its economic needs. The school owned acres of turpentine forests, a good investment. Outside labor had for a time to be brought in and Benson would not allow the usual concomitants, women and liquor. He saw his turpentine drip away one year. When I went over the place with him things were improving, but he had not the Northerner's keen efficiency, his work was severely criticized, and he died heartbroken. Probably no one could then have succeeded with it, but it was a brave experiment.

His father, hardheaded, matter of fact, had no use for philanthropy. He was one of the richest men in the country and employed white as well as colored help. I recall his drove of cattle as they stood in his spacious yard, the great bull among the cows. It was a Rosa Bonheur picture. He told me that at the end of the war he sat on the fence with the other colored boys and watched the Yankees march by. The soldiers called for them to come and follow and the other boys slipped off the fence and accepted the invitation. But he stayed behind. He had a hunch that he could get what he wanted at home.

Driving back to Alexander City in our open carriage, I experienced, not for the first time, the frightful character of Alabama's roads. The carriage tipped so that once I got out to see the angle at which we stood. It wasn't as bad from the ground as from the carriage and I stepped in again reassured. The mud on my boots, however, was not reassuring. Only mules could have pulled us up that hill through the mud. New England may be too stony, but it has not a treacherous soil where wheels sink in innocent-looking places and where gullies form overnight. No wonder each house stands like a wart on the face of the landscape.

At the end of two weeks, I said good-byes to Mr. and Mrs. Manning. Their hospitality was all that the South stands for. They gave me of their best. I never saw them again in their home, but Mr. Manning came more than once to the North and died there in 1931 of an incurable ailment.

Shortly after I returned to New York, a large crate with slats was left in my apartment, after I had paid a good many dollars in expressage. In it, crouched in a corner, was a strange, weasel-like animal. I surmised what it was but asked my friend, Thomas Bell, to identify it for me. As I had guessed, it was an opossum, sent by the Mannings because just before I left I said that I had never tasted one. I never tasted this. It was taken to a butcher's shop, but before execution it escaped into the neighboring backyards and a smart Southern colored boy caught it and ate it at home with the proper trimmings. I feel sure, had his family known it was mine, I should have been invited to the feast. But I don't yet know what opossum tastes like.

Manning also wrote a letter giving local news. It seems that, shortly after I left Alexander City, the Methodist church had a business meeting, at which the minister was reprimanded for having gone with me to the colored school. A motion was made to have his already small salary reduced. The minister did not recede from his position but made a rousing speech. He declared that he ought to have visited the colored school before and believed that it should be given more money. As to Miss Ovington, he was proud to have accompanied her to the school and to have met her. He would visit the Negro school whenever he wanted to.

Men like courage. The crowd raised his salary two hundred dollars.

While I went South to get Negro material, I was also deeply interested in the labor problem. The only people I found with a touch of radicalism were the old Populists. Why they have been ignored by historians, while the despoiled slaveholders are gushed over a little more with each new volume printed, I fail to understand. Were I an historian, I should write a history of the South since the Civil War which features the working class, white and colored, and which shows the efforts they have made through politics, and otherwise, to improve their condition. These efforts failed and so are easily forgotten. But Populism tried to help the agricultural laborer. In 1892, when Weaver ran on the ticket, the Populists polled a large Southern vote. When Tillman was elected governor by the Farmers' Alliance, T. Thomas Fortune wrote an article in the New York *Age* expressing appreciation of the interest the governor was taking in the workers of both races. Then, in 1896, Bryan was nominated on the Democratic ticket and the Populist party merged with the Democrats, a fatal move for the Southern proletariat.

At Calhoun I met Edward Chestnut, a white man from whom the school had bought its land. He was without race prejudice, eating with the colored teachers and helping the boys without patronizing them. His father had been a carriage builder, opposed to the war, who fought only ten days. When peace came he was bankrupt, having paid his all to keep out of what he believed to be a "rich man's war and a poor man's fight." His sons had little schooling, but the one who helped at Calhoun certainly had learned fundamental things, clear thinking, sobriety, sincerity. He had worked for the Populist party and told me of its hopes and its downfall.

I was a member of the Socialist party and looked up the one address I had, that of the state secretary who resided at Birmingham. I asked him to call on me at my hotel. He arrived and we sat on the balcony overlooking the busy lobby. He was pathetic. One eye was blind, he had lost his sight in an accident, he was undernourished and insufficiently clothed. He had joined the party from conviction and, when he became an active member, had lost everything. His wife had left him. His little girl was dead, and perhaps it was just as well, he thought; he could do nothing for her. He had been fired from his job and blacklisted. He was now printing a little paper for the party.

We talked of the class conflict, of internationalism, of the good time coming. I had heard Jack London and tried to make him feel the enthusiasm he had kindled in us all. We spoke of the Negro and with some pride he drew a letter from his pocket from a colored comrade. "They make good Socialists when they become members," he said. I read the letter from a Negro living still farther South and I remember that it ended with the usual slogan, "Yours for the revolution." The Socialists were hated because they received Negroes into the party on an equality. This brought indignities on men like himself. But he did not blame anyone, not his wife for leaving him, not his employer for discharging him. This was part of the meaning of revolution.

He got up to go and we shook hands. Evidently, he had something more to say and hardly knew how to say it. At length he phrased it. Had he been rude in any way? If so, he must ask to be excused. His life had been rough of late and he feared he might have forgotten how to behave to a woman. It was six months now since he had talked to any but men.

I reassured him of his unfailing courtesy and he went into the busy, restless lobby and out of sight. He left me with a heavy heart. What did we in New York know of party loyalty? Our locals talked revolution. This man lived it.

5 November 1932

Northern Alabama

When at Calhoun Colored School I went a number of times to Montgomery to visit the legislature, then in session—it met only once in four years. All the men were Democrats except two lonely Republicans. One came from a county in the center of the state that had gone Republican rather by chance, but the other came from Winston County in the north, always Union in its sentiment. Manning introduced me to these two men and I became so interested in the northern Republican county that I determined to visit there.

The member from Winston County was named Barton. He was sent primarily to defend the right of his county to elect its own officers. Looking for more party positions, the Democrats had introduced a bill to have the officers in Winston County appointed by the legislature instead of elected. The people of the county, being Republicans, were not capable of governing themselves. They had voted against the Civil War and had since been outcasts. As one of the members said in debate: "Winston County was in rebellion in 1860, and it is in rebellion still. It needs to be disciplined."

Mr. Barton was a conscientious member, always appearing at the sessions lest the bill against his county be introduced in his absence. He made many friends and succeeded in having the legislation withdrawn. I imagine he introduced no dangerous Republican doctrine.

After spending a short time in Birmingham among colored friends, I took the train for Winston County. I arrived in the morning at Barton's hometown, a straggling little settlement along the railroad track.

I sat on the porch most of the day, talking to the family, the boys were smart youngsters, and meeting some of Mr. Barton's friends. I think now that Manning had given him the idea that I had influence through Milholland with the Republican party. A vain

47

notion on his part! Anyway, I saw the leading men, the parson, who gave them a week of his time on his itinerant career, the doctor, the county leader.

The parson wore priest's clothes, high choker, and all in black. He was young, but assumed the air of the middle-aged ascetic.

The doctor was young also, and went about on horseback with his medicine in his saddlebags.

The Republican leader was a fine man with piercing eyes and an intelligent face. He spoke with feeling of the Negroes. "I do not want to know them socially," he said, "but I would not deny them their place in a republic. They need the vote as much as the white man."

He also spoke of the suffering in all that part of the country during the Civil War. Both sides ravaged it.

I heard the parson in a short evening service. A revival would follow later in the week. I wanted to put the young man into citizens' clothes and send him to a nice dance. Every natural emotion seemed thwarted. If one plays the part of a priest, one should be able to play it with the trappings, in a cathedral with noble music, swinging censers, and the comradeship of others of one's kind. The idea seemed to be, and I talked afterwards about it, that this man should be set off, quite alone.

I was very tired when the evening was over. I had had no chance to rest, because I did not know until night where I was to sleep. Then I found it was to be on the folding bed in the parlor. No washing arrangements were given me, and when I asked for them I was reluctantly handed the pitcher and bowl and towel that had done service all day on the porch. I was to be sure and put it back in the morning.

The most dramatic example of primitive ideas regarding cleanliness was at my next stop, the hotel at the county seat. A little girl, the daughter of my landlady, was deeply interested in my belongings. She examined my clothes, all my toilet articles, and then said, with finality: "You are a millionaire's daughter." I disclaimed the honor and asked her why she thought so. "Because," she answered, "you brought your own comb and brush."

Mr. Barton had business at the county seat and drove me there. The way was dreary, poor pinelands, poor fields, a few shabby, unpainted houses. But quite suddenly we came upon a neat house with flowers about it, a pruned grapevine, and a vegetable garden. "A German," Mr. Barton said, and told me of Cullman County, east of Winston, where a colony of Germans had settled and had brought fertility. How different our history would have been if the South had been settled by farmers like the Germans, or the "Dutch," as they call them in Pennsylvania. I've often thought that the English who settled this country, North as well as South, knew mighty little about farming.

I spent a day and two nights at the county seat, saw the grand jury sworn in—such long hair and scraggly beards and baggy clothes—and heard the judge's charge. I liked the judge, he was of the type of Chestnut and the Republican leader I had just met. He spoke in condemnation of a town that had a jail for Negroes that was worse than a pigpen. The audience all laughed at that. They had no Negroes in their part of the state, but they could have rivaled Scottsboro, I believe, if their passions had been roused.

I was a nine days' wonder to people. What was a New York lady doing in that remote place? Mr. Barton asked questions. Why wasn't I married? Did I dip snuff? At the hotel I was asked what I was selling. (My suitcase should have contained some new tonic.) They were curious but kindly. Not until I got on the train did I have an unpleasant experience. An ex-governor of a Southern state, an old man, was so insinuating, so anxious to continue in my company, that I ran from him when we reached Birmingham. Alone in my hotel room I began to feel frightened. I was an alien in this land. My only friends were also aliens, not citizens, and could not help me if I needed their help. I was glad when I was in the Pullman the next day, headed home.

I had meant to stay longer. I had seen the state with some thoroughness, Tuskegee (I have spoken of Washington), Selma, Talladega, Snow Hill, Lyman Ward's school for white boys, where a just attitude toward the Negro was stressed, and I would see Fisk on my way home. But at the last I was hurried. Home letters proposed a trip to Germany, Switzerland, and Italy. Of course, I wanted to go, but equally of course I was neglecting my investigations by going.

After leaving my settlement job, a salaried position, life began to be like the game of puss-in-the-corner. You remember, you stand in a corner of the room, and, when you get the chance, you rush to another corner before the person in the middle can tag you. There is always the likelihood of being tagged on the run. I had elected to do a piece of work on the Negro, but my book was not yet written, though my fellowship had expired some time before. I was receiving no remuneration, so at any minute I might be tagged by my family. This time nothing could have been pleasanter, and, as always, when abroad, I tried to see something of conditions in the working class. But I have never been able to see how a woman can bring up a family and carry a job. A man isn't expected to, doesn't attempt to. He does not have to assume new responsibility when he puts his key in the door. He's made much of, given the best chair and just what he likes to eat. But, when a woman with a family who goes out to work puts in her key, she simply assumes another responsibility. How can either piece of work be done continuously to her best ability? I know I can't manage it. I have not gone as far as I might have in my work for the Negro and I have led a snatchy home life.

However, I wasn't coerced. I did what I wanted to. Puss-in-the-corner is an exciting, entertaining game.

12 November 1932

The Migration of 1907–08 to New York

The next winter, 1907–08, found me living part of the time on San Juan Hill and entering upon new ventures.

Things were happening in the Negro world. The exodus to Harlem was under way. As the *New York Times* described it: "A constant stream of furniture loaded with household effects of a new colony of colored people who are invading the choice locality are pouring into the street. Another equally long procession moving in the other direction is carrying away the household goods of the whites from their homes of years."

Each group was bettering itself. The whites were moving into new law houses and the Negroes were obtaining better tenements in a better location than they had had before. I have watched this movement gathering strength until now it has pushed north into St. Nicholas Place and the upper reaches of Edgecombe Avenue, with the magnificent view over the city; south almost to Central Park; east beyond Fifth Avenue, and west until Riverside Drive itself begins to quiver a little with apprehension.

Much of the progress the colored man has made in New York within this century has come from settling in an attractive, healthy neighborhood. Great credit is due to the colored real estate men, to the late Philip A. Payton, to the Nalls, father and son, to others who took risks and braved the cupidity of the mortgage companies, finding the maligned, immigrant Jew more ready to give credit than the high-born, Nordic philanthropist.

Rents were high, so were taxes, but the Negro, driven from his old section, secured a place in the city where he could breathe and stretch himself.

Social service agencies were paying the colored race more attention. The Henry Street Settlement placed colored nurses in the Negro section, of course, drawing no hard and fast race lines. Frances Kellor, a college woman of unusual ability, an able sociolo-

51

gist, started a work to protect colored girls who were coming up from the South. Investigation showed that employment agencies were using such girls for immoral purposes. Richmond and Norfolk were in league with New York. This Society for the Protection of Colored Women did heroic work in exposing conditions, in securing more stringent laws regarding licenses, and in seeing that such laws were enforced.

Of special interest was a new Committee on the Economic Position of the Negro. Mr. William J. Schieffelin headed it. Mr. Oswald Garrison Villard was on it. Samuel Scottron, deceased, was its secretary. The committee hoped to do something toward securing better jobs for colored people. I cannot say that it got any number of Negroes positions, but it brought the attention of the public to the situation. Later this committee, with the Committee for the Protection of Colored Women, merged with the Urban League.

I was on these two committees and met many new people, colored and white. My book was moving along, somewhat slowly, but moving. Life was full of stimulation. Perhaps I should have been discouraged; the facts were discouraging enough, but, while there is work to do, discouragement is not the dominant note. It is when we read of terrible conditions, such as the world is suffering from now, and can do nothing that discouragement, even despair, sets in.

While busy with New York affairs, one of my colored friends, Dr. Verina Morton-Jones, a practicing physician of high standing, came to me with the plea that I do something for Brooklyn. It was my native town. I knew influential people there, why should I spend all of my energy on alien New York? I went with her through an old Negro section, Hudson Avenue, Fleet Street and Place, Prince Street, a neighborhood close to the city's shopping district, but unimproved, deplorable. Since then the Board of Health has torn down some of the houses for its building. I had known vaguely of the neighborhood but had never walked through it all before. I felt humiliated as I had after my first visit to Greenpoint. How little one knows of one's own city! Dr. Morton-Jones earnestly urged me to start a settlement in this section.

Impetuosity had its disadvantages. Had I realized all I was undertaking, I think I should have refused her plea. But I was pleased at the thought of being connected with a settlement again, though I would not be directing it. So, the two of us gathered together a board that elected me president; a house was rented and work begun. Remembering all that the Pratts had done in relieving me at Greenpoint of financial worries, I assumed with the board the responsibility of raising the money to run the settlement. The head worker would have enough to do to run the work.

Lincoln Settlement (the board chose the name, not I. I think Lincoln's name has been worked hard enough) came near dying "aborning." Just as we were getting into shape, the Cosmopolitan Club dinner came off, and the papers, particularly the Brooklyn papers, burst with the news of it. I had been a speaker at the dinner. Did I intend to use the new settlement house for other Cosmopolitan Club dinners? If so, support would be withdrawn. With the board I acquiesced in a denial that the new settlement would be used for a dinner club, and the money was subscribed.

I was still hoping to interest Mr. Phipps in a settlement house in New York, and I looked upon the Lincoln Settlement as less a place for residents than a community center for the neighborhood. We housed the kindergarten supported by the Kindergarten Association, and we started a much needed day nursery. We had two head workers, neither of whom was sufficiently trained to hold the place for long, when Dr. Morton-Jones made a sacrifice by giving up much of her practice and becoming herself the head worker.

Under her leadership the work grew, many volunteers were secured, clubs and classes met throughout the afternoon and evening. We bought the house which we had rented and with it a small playground. Ours was always a modest venture; our budget never reached over seven thousand. But such work as we did was conducted on the best lines that we knew. The settlement continues, the Urban League having taken over the financial management when I gave it up on moving to New York in 1923.

I did not find the children in the Brooklyn neighborhood as attractive as those on San Juan Hill. For the most part, they had been born and brought up in the city and their manners reminded me of Greenpoint. The boys were rough and the girls, too, were rough and saucy. Only the little tots, the day nursery children, showed that gentleness of manner that for so long distinguished Negroes.

John Quincy Adams, more than a hundred years ago, said of them that they were the only well-bred people in America.

The need of self-protection led our children to be as tough as their neighborhood. As one little girl said to me: "I keeps away from the white girls at school. My mother tells me to smack anyone as calls me 'nigger' and I ain't looking for trouble."

These generalizations, of course, admit of many exceptions. Given an incentive, especially given the incentive of beauty, and the rough child became intent, changed. Some years after our work was started, an artist and teacher, Robert Coady, entered a mission on Hudson Avenue (how disappointed we were, when we found out about it, that he had not knocked at our door) and asked whether he might teach the children to paint and draw. Permission was given, a room provided, and the boys, many from our settlement, gathered together. Their teacher intruded himself very little. He gave them materials—crayons, watercolors, and oil—and told them to paint anything that they liked. I remember one little boy who always lay on the floor, flat on his stomach, and painted ships on blue seas. Noble seas they were and noble ships. Others made canvases filled with figures. My impression is that no boy was over twelve.

Mr. Coady brought his boys' work to the attention of his friends, and the need of a better exhibition place was felt. Largely through the instrumentality of Mrs. James Weldon Johnson, an exhibit was held on Fifth Avenue and was well attended. The press gave it notice and in some cases high praise. *The Survey* magazine reproduced one of the pictures in color. It was called "Ham and Eggs" and showed a long table filled with people, each at his seat, the figures handled in a masterful way. Mr. Coady said the Negro boys' work was superior to anything he had seen in his other classes. For myself, I have never seen this child-work excelled except once at the Brooklyn Museum, where the work came from Austria.

The class stopped before long. Mr. Coady was ill and later died. No one came to fill his place and the boys dropped their crayons and paints and went back to horseplay. That Hudson Avenue, with its tumble-down wooden houses, its elevated shaking through the streets, threatening to shake the houses down, its dirty babies, its bedraggled girls, its mischief-making boys, should have produced such color and line, such creative imagination, seemed a miracle. And yet I suppose the miracle is always here if someone will come to call it forth.

As I have counted off the months and seen my story approaching September 1908 I have wondered how I could tell of the most important happening of my life. I have shown my Negro work—investigation, travel, social service. It interested me, but it was not wholly satisfying. Socialism had taught me to look below the surface of a problem to the cause. Was I doing anything for the fundamental cause of the race's condition? The Negro was living under democratic government, but he was treated as a subject, and to be subject to another race in a democracy is worse than to be under a despotism. I felt this keenly as I read an account of the Springfield riots in the *Independent* for September 3, 1908. A mob of the town's "best citizens" had raged for two days, had killed and wounded scores of Negroes, and had driven thousands from the city. And nothing was done about it. I had seen the story in the daily papers and now read it again. At length I came to the last page. This is what it said:

> Either the spirit of the abolitionists, of Lincoln and Lovejoy, must be revived and we must come to treat the Negro on a plane of absolute political and social equality, or Vardaman and Tillman will soon have transferred the race war to the North—Yet who realizes the seriousness of the situation, and what large and powerful body of citizens is ready to come to their aid?

Here was the first person who had sent a challenge to white and colored to battle, as the abolitionists had battled, for the full rights of the Negro. Drums beat in my heart. I sat down and wrote to the author of the article. His name was William English Walling.

19 November 1932

The NAACP Begins

William English Walling, whose article on the Springfield Riots so impressed me, is of Kentucky origin, a Southerner born and familiar with the Southern view of the race question. I knew him as a Socialist. His wife, Anna Strunsky, had shown interest in the Niagara Movement. The two had been together in Russia, where Mrs. Walling had been imprisoned for a short time, accused of revolutionary activities. On returning to America, with Mr. Walling she went to Springfield, and they both felt that the prejudice they saw against the Negro was worse than the prejudice they had seen in Russia against the Jew. In Russia the Czarist government worked up a pogrom. But no one outside was needed to work up this American pogrom, and Mrs. Walling found only one person who spoke in sympathy with the Negro in all Springfield—a Salvation Army worker.

Mr. Walling and I did not meet to plan for that "large and powerful body of citizens" who should work together in the spirit of the abolitionists until early in January. I went to his apartment on the day agreed upon and met Henry Moskowitz, later active in municipal reform. I should have met Charles Edward Russell, but he was detained at the last minute. We spent the afternoon discussing the race question and deciding on people to form a committee to start the movement he had outlined. Of course, Oswald Garrison Villard's name occurred at once, and William Ward's and Hamilton Holt's, the two editors of the *Independent;* Bishop Walters was the first Negro to join with us. We decided that we would choose February twelfth, the centenary of Lincoln's birth, for a pronouncement on the race question and a call for a conference.

A small committee soon got to work, and Mr. Villard drafted the Call. It was in his forceful English, with an emotional appeal. It recited the chief wrongs under which the Negro suffered and called

56

for a conference "for the discussion of present evils, the voicing of protests and the renewal of the struggle for civil and political liberty."

It was most important, for the sake of publicity, to have this Call signed by people of national reputation. In the short time we had I think we did very well. There were some ludicrous omissions, notably that of Moorfield Storey, but our list was impressive. We were headed by Jane Addams, and among other social workers were Lillian D. Wald, Florence Kelly, and Mary McDowell. Among newspaper editors and publicists were Villard, Holt, Ward, Samuel Bowles of the Springfield *Republican*, Lincoln Steffens, and Charles Zeublin. Parkhurst, Peters, Holmes, Wise, and Hirsch were among the preachers. The two college presidents were Mary E. Wooley of Mt. Holyoke and C. F. Thwing of Western Reserve. Of course John E. Milholland's name was there, and we were proud to have that of William Dean Howells. Seven Negroes signed: W. E. B. Du Bois, Ida Wells Barnett, William L. Bulkley, E. H. Clement, Bishop Alexander Walters, and the Reverends Francis Grimke and Milton Waldron.

Owing to the excellent work of the committee, especially of Mr. Walling and Mr. Villard, the Call was given wide publicity, and more than any one thing made the coming conference a success.

The conference opened on May 29, with a reception at the Henry Street Settlement, where Miss Wald was then, and often afterwards, our cordial hostess and where Fanny Garrison Villard, Garrison's daughter, received. The next morning the sessions opened in the hall of the Charity Organization Building and lasted, morning, afternoon, and evening for two days.

This was the first and last time that we published our proceedings in book form. They are still interesting reading and much that was said then could be said today. It was not a conference of opinion so much as a conference of facts. And the speakers kept to the ten- and fifteen-minute rule and managed to say a great deal in their time. (In a whisper I would guess that this was because the majority were white.) We had a morning given over to ethnology, with Livingston Farrand, now president of Cornell, and Burt Wilder, also of Cornell, the greatest American authority on man's brain structure. Professor Wilder asked to be allowed to leave his subject for a few moments and gave an exquisite tribute to the Massachusetts Fifty-fourth and Fifty-fifth regiments (he was on the medical staff of the Fifty-fifth). Then we turned to sociology, with Dr. Du Bois relating a series of facts regarding labor and prejudice and Professor

Seligman of Columbia telling us to remember that mankind moves
very slowly. We had John Dewey on education and a long list of
other well-known people, twenty-four speakers, with discussion
following the speaking.

The familiar socialist and liberal policies were outlined by their
adherents as they would be today. The necessity of joining forces
with labor was emphasized. On the whole there was a considerable
volume of opinion that, if our would-be organization worked hard
and faithfully and uncompromisingly, we could improve conditions
along the lines of disfranchisement, segregation, and mob violence.

But, apart from the speeches, the conference was of great
value in bringing the two races together. We were together pretty
much all the time those two days. We secured a private dining room
in a hotel on Union Square, and there, from soup to coffee, the
debates were carried on and ideas exchanged. During the first
evening's discussion, when someone said we had had enough agitation, Mr. Russell replied as follows:

> I can't think we have had too much agitation. I have had more edu-
> cation on this question since ten o'clock this morning than I have had
> before in all the rest of my life, and I think I have been a pretty close
> observer. I tell you that what I have heard today has opened up an
> entirely new horizon to me. . . . Now there are only a few of us here,
> but it is a beginning and every great movement has to have its begin-
> ning, and if we will strike hands together and increase our numbers
> and look forward, we will have our remedy.

This of the conference. But what went on behind the scenes
where a few of us were trying to launch successfully what we felt in
our hearts would be an all-important movement?

I think it's legitimate now to raise the curtain a little. Our controversy was a part of the time in which we lived and was inevitable.
It centered about Booker T. Washington. Was it possible to build up
any organization, to get support for what we knew would become
expensive work, without his sanction? Must we not at least ask him
to be on our committee? We were drafting resolutions to be voted
on at the last conference session. Those resolutions ended with a list
of members for a permanent committee. Could we ignore the man
who was unquestionably the most influential and the most famous
Negro living?

I thought then, and I still think, that Washington would not have come in with us if he had been asked. Of course, he could have joined the committee to kill it, but, if he was like every other Negro I knew, he would have rejoiced at the thought that there was a group of people, of both races, prepared to battle for the Negroes' rights. And what I felt keenly was that, if we put on his name, we should not have the support of the Negroes whom we absolutely needed. We would start out under suspicion. The matter was thrashed back and forth, and in the end we made a compromise. If Washington's name was omitted, the radicals agreed to have a few conservative names on the committee and not to include Washington's bitterest enemies. So, the last night we went before the conference with very strong resolutions but with a committee whose Negro members represented various schools of thought.

These were the Negroes put upon the general committee: New York, the Rev. W. H. Brooks (for years a devoted member of the board), Bishop Alexander Walters, Dr. William L. Bulkley; Brooklyn, Dr. Owen M. Waller; Boston, Maria Baldwin and Archibald Grimké; Wilberforce, W. S. Scarborough; Chicago, Ida Wells Barnett, Dr. C. E. Bentley; Philadelphia, R. R. Wright, Jr., and William Sinclair; Washington, Mary Church Terrell, Milton Waldron, and L. M. Hershaw; Atlanta, W. E. B. Du Bois; and Manassas, Leslie P. Hill.

Among the whites Moorfield Storey's name appeared for the first time and Albert Pillsbury's. So did Paul Kennaday's. It was not until 1910 that we found J. E. Spingarn.

We lived through the last meeting, but only, I am convinced, because Charles Edward Russell was in the chair. The majority of the people launching the movement were white and therefore under suspicion. Were they going to be namby-pamby at the last, as so many whites before them had been, and counsel halfway measures? The resolutions demanded the ballot, the same education for colored as the white, and the enforcement of the Fourteenth and Fifteenth Amendments. They were debated and amended and discussed word by word. Some of the discussion was valuable, some of it was not. There are always cranks who get into such a meeting. But about midnight the resolutions were passed, including the names of the new committee, which was called a committee of forty and of which Mr. Walling was chairman. There was a little angry talk in the aisles when we disbanded, but I think we were commended by the majority.

It was good to get out into the cool night. A group of my friends piled into a touring car and waved me to join them, but I shook my head. I needed to be alone. I was exhausted physically, mentally, emotionally. I had no strength left with which to celebrate.

There was another reason for my exhaustion. My father had died a few days before the conference began. I could only feel thankful for his sake, for his illness had been painful and hopeless from the start. But the sense of loneliness was great. We had always been close to one another, seeming to understand one another without effort. The day after the conference I went with my mother to the country. By letter I learned of the thunderous recriminations that fell upon Mr. Russell's and Mr. Walling's ears.

For I have not told quite the whole story; Ida Wells Barnett's name was omitted in the committee's list brought before the conference. But she got it put on in the next few days. And there it stands, where it ought to be. She was a great fighter, but we knew that she had to play a lone hand. And if you have too many players of lone hands in your organization, you soon have no game.

26 November 1932

The West Indies

The winter after my father's death my mother was seriously ill with pneumonia, and on her recovery we decided to spend the rest of the winter in a milder climate. We chose Jamaica and sailed in February, accompanied by my brother-in-law, an artist.

Jean Webster, author of *Daddy Long Legs*, found Jamaica, as she sailed by the mountains to Kingston Harbor, more beautiful than any she had ever seen, not excepting the harbor of Naples. I felt the same when I saw the Blue Mountains, in the early morning, covered with that indescribably pearly haze that one sees only in the tropics. Jamaica's only rival that I have seen is Madeira.

The island is ravishing from the land as well as from the sea. It is somewhat the size of Long Island, which it resembles about as much as Hamlet resembles an editorial in the *New York Times*. Jamaica has high mountains; broad, rushing rivers; tangled forests filled with tropical birds; immense ferns; and great, crawling parasites. On the one point where Long Island might enter into competition, the seacoast, Jamaica has lovelier harbors, and no northern sea has the dazzling color of the sea in the tropics.

I was so entranced with nature that at first I scarcely noticed the people. Moreover, I had Gosse's *Birds of Jamaica*, and turned to identifying new hummingbirds, doves, and birds with such fascinating names as Hopping Dick, Banana Quit, Green Tody.

But my artist brother-in-law soon taught me to watch the countrywomen as they came swinging down the road to market, their baskets on their heads. Their dark skins, purple lips, brilliant eyes were in harmony with the tropic sunshine. We did not admire the men so much, though occasionally we saw one with fine physique, but then the men were less in evidence than the women. They stayed at home to work the land, while the women carried the produce to market, having the more interesting time of the two.

"Look here," my artist brother-in-law said one day, "you are

61

attacking this matter of Negro equality the wrong way. Get a law passed that everyone must go nude and the superiority of the Negro is proved."

No one would have been more shocked at this solution than the dignified women who were to benefit by it. They were so modest that they could not be persuaded to pose except when fully clothed.

We stayed in Kingston for a week, went to Port Antonio across the mountains and back by the coast, spent another week in the hills at Mandeville, and then to Montego Bay, where we lingered until it was imperative that we return to Kingston to try on the exquisite linen dresses being made for us and to take the steamer home.

Claude McKay, in his early verse, described the loving faithfulness of the Negro peasant, his patient endurance of poverty, and his affection for his home. I saw this type at Mandeville, where I went to a colored church. In the front row were two young men in policemen's uniforms. In the course of his sermon the minister looked down at them and spoke of their having recently been chosen for their positions. The reason he gave was that they had the peace of God in their hearts. The young men showed no self-consciousness and looked as though the words were true. There was something touching and very remote from New York in the thought that a policeman had been chosen for his job because in his heart was the peace of God.

In talking to my landlady when I returned to my modest hotel, I learned that the young policemen would have little to do. The community was law-abiding. About the only crime was petty larceny, chiefly manifested in the stealing of yams. "And I suppose as long as the world lasts," she concluded, "the lazy man will steal the yams belonging to his industrious neighbor."

As those familiar with the British West Indies know, the population is divided into three classes, white, colored, and black. The whites, about two percent, have all the best jobs. Next come the colored, who work as clerks in stores and have the best jobs after the whites have taken their pick. And last come the overwhelming mass of the population, the blacks, who do all the hard work.

Our dressmaker was a colored woman living in one of the few beautiful houses left after the earthquake. When I first met her the rector of the English church was taking his leave, and his manners were those of a man speaking to his equal. I had an introduction to the principal of a large school, a charming colored man, and spent an afternoon on his tennis court, where white and colored were playing together.

The English long ago learned that the way to rule a conquered people is to encourage caste. By dividing their subjects among themselves, they can act as judges and arbitrators, positions which even their enemies admit they fill well. This island has lost its native population, and a handful of English are ruling the descendants of former slaves, partly by giving privileges to the lighter-colored class, the class with English blood. Thus, the tendency of the educated Negroes is to try to get lighter. To mix with the black is to lose a favorable status.

Many privileges are granted the colored and socially they are on a precarious borderline. I was struck with certain beautiful girls, undoubtedly with a touch of colored blood, who were often at the hotel with young Englishmen. I was told they came from their homes and returned to their homes—usually—but they were playing a game that often ended with heartbreak. For such women to marry black men was unthinkable.

Marcus Garvey, with this background, tried to divide colored and black in the United States. He created bitter feeling, but he left things much as they had been.

Educational methods have doubtless changed, but in 1910 the student showing marked ability was trained for Oxford or Cambridge and seemed singularly ignorant of his own land. I was provoked because he could recite to you of nightingales and doves, but he didn't know the names of a dozen of his own birds. Whatever enterprise he had was not used to improve conditions in his own land but was concerned in getting away from it as soon as possible.

We used to drive in the afternoon. I was always surprised that the native population had done nothing to provide refreshment. We were in an English land and afternoon tea would have been greatly appreciated.

A Yankee would have had a teahouse at the end of every drive and have made money when the season was over. But neither colored nor black took advantage of our thirst. I used to recall a very successful teahouse on Mt. Desert, Maine, run by a native, where you could have all the tea and toast and marmalade that you wanted for a quarter. In Jamaica you could get the best English tea without paying duty, could pluck oranges from the trees, and could get sugar from a nearby mill. You could have asked a shilling for what would not have cost you more than two pence. But you didn't use two pence worth of energy; instead, you took the boat to New York. And New York taught you nothing, for you didn't take a later boat home and start the teahouse with northern capital.

However, if the number of business opportunities that the Negroes fail to seize, coupled with those opportunities which they seize and then lose because of lack of method and promptness and shrewd intelligence, were all put together, they would reach from Jamaica to the United States!

Of all the Negroes working today to better the race I think Albon L. Holsey of the Business League most heroic, and I pity him the most.

English Walling had given me an introduction to Sydney Olivier, the Governor-General of Jamaica. I knew Olivier's book, *White Capital and Colored Labor,* and counted it the best book in English on the subject. He had an international viewpoint and great knowledge. The English on the island, I found, did not care for him. The reasons given were that he did not drive out in state and had whiskers. He grew increasingly unpopular after Bernard Shaw had visited him, for Shaw was merciless in his ridicule of the British colonial.

I sent my letter of introduction through the mail and received a reply, which an orderly, on horseback, left at the hotel desk. This should have been form enough even for an Englishman. I accepted the date appointed, in the afternoon, and ordered a carriage, as the local cabs were not much to look at. But, as I was going down the hotel stairs, dressed in my best, some tourists jumped into my carriage and went off. I had little time to spare and took the first hack I could get, the oldest carriage, horse, and driver, I feel sure, in Jamaica. The driver, a very aged Negro, was excited at going to the Governor's and whipped up his horse until I cried out for mercy. We reached the executive mansion in safety and just on time.

Mr. Olivier (he had not yet been made a lord) was a shy man, but entirely friendly. He told me a good deal about conditions not only in the West Indies but in India, where he had held a government position. We had tea together, the two of us, and I felt both instructed and honored. The governor himself took me to my carriage and so excited my driver that he nearly dumped me out into the road. He made a sharp curve, the governor shouted at him, he drove worse than ever, and I expected to be thrown on the ground, not a serious fall, as it was a low victoria. But I got away safely at last. I did not feel kindly toward those tourists.

April arrived and with it mosquitoes. Flies you have always with you at Jamaica, and if you go near the cattle a particularly vicious tick burrows under your skin. So, we left our lovely island and sailed up north to strike a blizzard. The time was over for viewing beauty. We must return to the city's tumult and work.

3 December 1932

Early Years of the NAACP and the Urban League

$\mathcal{I}$ have written of my trip to the West Indies. I returned to New York in April to find on the minute book of the National Negro Committee (soon to become the National Association for the Advancement of Colored People) this item: "That the entire matter of the coming conference go over until Miss Ovington's return." Lincoln Settlement was also waiting for me to raise some money. My work was cut out for me.

Like all associations pledged to unpopular causes, our committee was at first manned entirely by volunteers. Soon Frances Blascoer was engaged as secretary to the board and its chairman. It was not until the conference of 1910 that we assumed a considerable responsibility and called Dr. W. E. B. Du Bois from Atlanta University to take the position of Director of Publicity and Research. Also that year we left the Liberal Club, where we had held our business meetings, and had offices in the *Evening Post* building, downtown New York, at 20 Vesey Street.

Our tiny rooms were used, one by the *Crisis*, one by the NAACP. One day we were told to move to 26 Vesey Street, a large loft building owned by the *Evening Post*, next door, where we should have more space and the chance to expand. Mr. Villard, then president of the Evening Post Company, succeeded Mr. Walling in 1911 as chairman of the board, and we were at Vesey Street at his invitation. Naturally there was nothing for it but to move. I liked it; I hated crowded quarters, but the two clerks at the *Crisis*, we had two by then, Lottie Jarvis and Frank M. Turner, still ably handling our accounts, looked grave. Dr. Du Bois was away. How should they move his things without disturbing their order? File cases were piled on file cases, papers put into boxes, and, with the velocity that movers can show, we were whisked from one building to the other. When the director of publicity and research returned we all kept out of his way as much as possible. It was "research" for him, indeed! I expect he's looking for some of those papers still!

Shortly after the second conference we changed our name from the National Negro Committee to the National Association for the Advancement of Colored People. No one liked the new name. It was so cumbersome, but we couldn't find a better, and, though for two or three years afterwards we kept making suggestions to change or shorten it, it still stands with all its eight words. Even initialed it's too long.

The Crisis, which started in November 1910, was happily christened after Lowell's poem, "The Present Crisis" (dated December 1844). Every schoolboy ought to know this poem, with its last verse starting: "New occasions teach new duties." But as, probably, not one in a million does, I give the verse, which we quoted when the magazine was named:

> Once to every man and nation
>   comes the moment to decide.
> In the strife of Truth with Falsehood,
>   on the good or evil side;
> Some great cause, God's new Messiah,
>   offering each the bloom or blight,
> Parts the goats upon the left hand,
>   and the sheep upon the right,
> And the choice goes by forever
>   'twixt that darkness and that light.

We had an enormous program before us. An association pledged to advance the cause of Colored People! One could do almost anything under that title. In the first place, "colored" could be construed loosely and include other races than Negroes. Only about a year before one of our founders, Charles Edward Russell, made a strong plea to the board that we espouse the cause of the Philippinos on the Pacific Coast. We decided against this, as we had earlier decided against espousing the cause of the East Indian. But, though a national organization, we went past our boundary line, calling Pan African Congresses and entering heartily into the Haitian struggle for Independence. Then, how should "advancement" be construed? It might include anything from helping a boy through college to securing the vote in Georgia. What was our rightful field?

I hope we shall never answer this question dogmatically, but this "new abolitionism," a phrase J. E. Spingarn has coined for us, was first of all to be concerned with securing greater freedom for a proscribed race.

Fortunately, early in our career a large field of "advancement" was taken over by another organization (the Urban League), whose representatives met in our office in 1911, where together we mapped out our boundaries. With Professor George Haynes, then of Fisk University, Professor Seligman of Columbia, Elizabeth Walton, and others, we discussed our problems and made clear our purposes. Our visitors represented the merger of the National Committee on the Protection of Negro Women and the New York Committee on Improving Industrial Conditions among Negroes (I have already written of both of these) and had plans for other economic and social service activities.

We were organized to promote the Negro's rights as a citizen, to uphold the Thirteenth, Fourteenth, and Fifteenth Amendments, and to defend him against race prejudice. As an example: they would have a committee on housing and would endeavor to secure better homes for the colored. We would defend the Negro when he entered his home and the white man bombed it. Cases of bombing were going on at that time in Kansas City, Mo., and our always efficient, loyal branch was starting there. So, we made our platforms and have adhered to them. We rejoiced as the Urban League started its career, a career that has brought innumerable benefits to the American Negro.

The wisdom of our movement was proved by its immediate popularity among the population whose cause it espoused. Boston, Washington, Chicago at once formed branches. Our third conference was in Boston, the sessions held in historic Park Street Church. There were white people there, Moorfield Storey, our president from our inception until his death, the Bradfords, Louds, Hallowells, Adelene Moffat, and among the Negroes, Mr. and Mrs. Butler R. Wilson, who at once joined with us, and helped not only the national office but built up a formidable organization to combat growing prejudice in their own city.

Our fourth conference was at Chicago, where the late Charles Bentley and Ida Wells Barnett were prominent. They made the mistake of taking Ethical Culture Hall, much too small for our meetings, for we were growing fast in popularity. Mary McDowell, then, as always, welcomed us, and we had a reception at Hull House at which Jane Addams was present and where Abdul Baha made a wonderful speech. The NAACP likes to remember that it called the attention of this great religious leader to conditions among the Negroes of the United States.

Our first legal case of importance strikingly illustrated what was before us: a tenant in trouble with his landlord; a sheriff entering the tenant's house without a warrant; shooting; the sheriff killed; the tenant sentenced to death. This was the substance of the Pink Franklin case, which, with the aid of Gonzales, editor and writer of *Gullah Tales*, we won, securing a commutation to life imprisonment. Some years later Pink Franklin was released. A similar case, that of Steve Williams, occurred the same year in Arkansas.

A New York branch, under the leadership of Mr. J. E. Spingarn, tested the civil rights law of the state and won many cases against discrimination in theaters and restaurants. White and colored entered into this civic work.

We were desperately poor, and, when Miss Blascoer left us in the autumn of 1910, I took the secretaryship for the winter and spring. It was then that we began our anti-lynching campaign, a campaign that went on for fifteen years and is not over yet.

There were three of us white women working on this gruesome subject, Mary Maclean, regular writer on the *New York Sunday Times* (from Nassau, where she had learned to ignore color), Martha Gruening, and myself. One Sunday morning Mrs. Maclean and I made up our first anti-lynching pamphlet. It must be at the printer's the next day, so we sat in the Vesey Street office pasting pictures of men tortured to death.

One postcard, it had been sent to John Haynes Holmes as a warning of what a "nigger-lover" might expect from the South, showed the body of a Negro and back of it, facing the camera, were the white lynchers. This had gone through the mails. Those men who so willingly stood for their pictures had no fear that any court would ever try them, much less convict them.

Across the street was St. John's Church, one of New York's oldest places of worship. Through our open window we could hear the people singing, and, as we pasted one gruesome picture after another, telling the story of the white man's thirst for vengeance and love of torture, we heard the Gloria and Te Deum raised in honor of a crucified God.

During this year the Coatesville, Pennsylvania, lynching occurred and Mr. Villard felt that no expense should be spared to get a conviction. A Negro had been burned to death in a Northern state. We, as Northerners, must do our utmost to bring the perpetrators of the crime to justice. So, we all tried to raise money, and Martha Gruening and I attended to the details of our first important anti-lynching meeting, held at Ethical Culture Hall, with John Lovejoy Elliott presiding.

Indifference is harder to meet than prejudice. New Yorkers were not interested in anti-lynching. Nearly all believed that, when a Negro was lynched, it was for the crime of rape, and, while mob violence was wrong, it was easily excused. We tried to get men prominent in politics, orthodox religious leaders, platform speakers. They were sorry but they could not come. We ended by turning to our own group and John Haynes Holmes and Stephen S. Wise filled our program. They were young men then, newly come to New York, their reputation in the making. They showed their calibre that night. John Lovejoy Elliott presided. It was a thrilling gathering, and the subscriptions secured started our anti-lynching fund.

The best was none too good for the Coatesville work, so William J. Burns was engaged at what then seemed an enormous sum, to find evidence against at least some members of the lynching mob.

This was my one and only experience with a detective agency, and I found it inconclusive and not nearly so interesting as a mystery story. Burns may have been a great detective, but in our case he did nothing that showed especial intelligence. Two of his men, heavy-jawed, strikingly unimaginative-looking, opened a restaurant at Coatesville, hoping to learn something from the talk of the patrons. They heard shocking details of the burning, the screams of the victims, the smell of the flesh, but they got nothing to be used at court. Mary Maclean, who went there first, learned more of the inner workings of the affair, the responsibility of people higher up— the people who supply fuel for the mob and then stay primly at home when the actual lynching occurs—than the detectives ever showed us. In England there may be men with the acumen of Sherlock Holmes, with the infinite patience of Dr. Thorndike, but they weren't around the Burns's investigation at Coatesville.

Burns himself disappointed me. He dropped in now and then to get his money and once he was talkative and told me the method of approach in a case like ours. You should go to the town and make friends with the men who constituted the mob. Show your sympathy with them, revile the "nigger," worm yourself into men's confidence. Gradually, you will learn the true facts of the case. When a man is a little tipsy, loquacious, he may tell you all. Then you clap the handcuffs on him.

How much pleasanter the task of the detective in fiction!

I completed my promised time as secretary and May Childs Nerney came to us and instituted more business-like methods than I had ever compassed. That summer I dropped responsibility and went to the Races' Congress in London.

10 December 1932

Studio Days

$\mathcal{I}$ speak of my studio because it was in a studio building, not because I, or anyone else, drew or painted there. But for about ten years I had a sort of glorified office in Brooklyn. It was only two minutes from the Hotel St. George, where my mother and I then lived. At one end of the room my secretary, for the majority of the time, Alice L. Brown, kept her typewriter and the letter files. She helped me more than I can ever express. At the other end I had my business desk and, behind a bookcase, a kitchenette. In between, it was a long, irregular space, were more books and chairs and a comfortable sofa. There was a high north window back of my desk, and the whole west side was full of windows, with a view of the river. Altogether, a place that one might legitimately call a studio, whether or not anything artistic was done in it.

In 1911 my book on the status of the Negro in New York was published by Longmans, Green and Co. I called it *Half a Man*, taking the title from a statement I heard a young college student make: "My father comes north in the summer to be a man. No, (correcting himself), half a man. A Negro is wholly a man only in Europe." I contributed to magazines and had a heavy correspondence. One winter I had a weekly class in current events, reviewing events from the standpoint, as I rather grandiosely expressed it, of democracy. It meant studying the *Nation* and the *Survey* and the out-of-the-way corners of the *New York Times* pretty thoroughly. But the war came, and democracy was the last thing anyone could talk about, except the president.

I did all my Lincoln Settlement work in my studio, and Alice Brown took my dictation, kept my correspondence, and deposited hundreds of begging letters in the post office. I enjoyed writing our annual reports, using *Crisis* babies for the covers.

I had, and still have, a great many people ask me to look at manuscripts of plays or stories or poems. I dread to open such a

72

manuscript, for so many feel that they are called and so very few are ever chosen by the publishers. One day I had an agreeable surprise. Dr. Morton-Jones asked me to look at the children's stories of a young girl who was helping her at the settlement, Augusta Bird (now Augusta Courtney, a widow with two adorable children). I found her material not sufficiently worked up—she has never yet been able to more than outline her idea—but it was amazingly interesting stuff. When I met her and saw her golden-red hair and white skin, I realized that she had more to tell than she had written. But her children's stories were very good.

A few years after this, a publisher, Harcourt, Brace and Company, asked me to help in the compilation of a first-year high school reader for colored schools. Everything in the reader was to be the work of the Negro. I found plenty of biography, travel, folklore, poetry, but I had no luck with children's stories. After much searching, I discovered one of Paul Laurence Dunbar's and one of Angelina Grimke's. That surely was not enough. So, I turned to the NAACP office, where Augusta Bird was then working, and asked her for a child's story. She wrote an excellent one. I asked another of our office force, Lillian Witten; she gave me two. I turned to Walter White, then unknown as a writer (the *Fire in the Flint* had not been published); he wrote one. They were all satisfactory to the expert with whom I was working. I wonder, what other small office could have shown so much talent?

My studio was a place for play as well as work. People from out of town learned to make their way to "Brooklyn," for I had a card printed describing how to get to 246 Fulton Street. Brooklynites will appreciate my difficulty in trying to describe how to turn on issuing from the subway stairways at Borough Hall. Even New Yorkers condescended to make the trip. Many friends on the NAACP board and members of the Cosmopolitan Club came over to supper. We were not always discussing the race problem. I can see Margaret Wycherley, one of the few really distinguished actresses in America, teaching LeRoy Scott, the novelist, a new dance step. Sometimes I had a visit from a well-seasoned traveller. Dr. W. H. Sheppard brought me some lovely things from the Congo, and described to a group of us his exposure of the Congo atrocities and the dangers through which he passed. But the guest who gave me the most romantic picture of faraway scenes was the Liberian, Dihdwo Twe.

Twe had been educated in an English school in Liberia and in a boys' school in this country and was planning to return shortly to his native land. I met him in 1910. He liked to talk of Africa, and I, feeling that I was getting information firsthand, liked to listen. I have an idea now that he was one of those people who improve a story with each telling. He loved to boast that he was a Kru. "We do the work," he would say. "When England or France takes a piece off the coast of Liberia, they take it, not for the land, but for the Krus who live on it." One afternoon he entertained a group of my friends by telling how he had received his name. I had remarked that I found it impossible to remember where the "W" was placed. "That might be one reason," he answered, "that the teachers wanted it changed at school." It seemed that at the English school he had attended all the boys took Christian names, and he had been told one day that he must give up Dihdwo Twe and be called James Brown. He went home to tell his mother about it. She shook her head. And then he learned the significance of his real name.

His mother had made a love match, leaving her home to marry a man of whom her people did not approve. "My father," Twe said, "did not have much property. He was a dreamer, a philosopher." He won his bride against the wishes of her parents and they ran away and lived far down the coast. For many months the two families heard nothing from one another. Then one day Twe's grandmother learned that her daughter had a son. "I must go and see the grandson that has been born," she told her husband. He put no obstacle in her way, so she started on her journey.

She walked down the coast for many days and at length came to the town where her daughter lived. "They have a time of day among our people," Twe explained, "when the mothers all sit outside their huts to wash their babies. It was then that my grandmother entered my mother's village to find her daughter. My mother rose from where she sat washing her baby and placed it in her mother's arms. The older woman fondled it and asked. 'Is it named?' My mother answered. 'No.' 'Then,' said my grandmother, 'we will call it Dihdwo Twe,' which means 'Peace is planted between us.' And can you wonder," Twe asked, as he finished his story, "that I did not want to change Dihdwo Twe for James Brown?"

He did not change it, though he had his hands full fighting the boys who would call him James. At length a bishop came along with a sense of the appropriate and told him he should remain Dihdwo Twe.

Twe had his father's dreamy nature. When he returned to Liberia, he had one hundred and twenty-five dollars of mine to be spent for curios. The curios never arrived. He had to go into the bush for them and the trip was dangerous. But he went and returned and still no curios came. Some years later, one of Twe's friends wrote me asking that he might call. He came and, with sparkling eyes and smiling lips, told me that Twe was going to send me my money. "When?" I asked. All the light went out of his face. What an unkind thing to say! He did not know when he would send it, but Twe had told him to give me the message. He was disappointed in me, and I continued to be disappointed, for neither curios nor money ever came.

If Dihdwo Twe did not like the name of Brown, it became very dear to me. Among my frequent visitors was the young artist, who for a time was well-known in the Negro world, Richard Lonsdale Brown.

In 1910, when Mr. Villard and I were working in the newly organized NAACP, he gave me a letter from the artist George de Forest Brush, asking me if I would take up the business mentioned in it. It told of a young colored artist, Richard Brown, from Charleston, West Virginia, who had recently come to New York with some excellent sketches. I called upon Mr. Brush in his picturesque studio on MacDougall Alley and saw his pictures. They were lovely things, trees and melting skies, alive in form and color. Mr. Brush was deeply impressed with them. "He is no more than a boy," he said, "and he came into my studio, shy, discouraged. He had brought his sketches under his arm to New York, and when not in one of our great galleries was spending his time trying to sell them. No one wanted even to look at them. He was poor; he was colored. Could one have greater handicaps?" Mr. Brush welcomed him to his studio and looked with interest and appreciation at his work. "Can I ever be an artist?" Richard asked when he had shown all he had. The answer was, "You are an artist."

Then came a short success. My brother gave him a gallery at Ovington's for a week in which to show his work. Mary Maclean, one of the regular editors of the *New York Times*, and a loyal NAACP worker, wrote him up in the *Times* the Sunday before the exhibition opened. Crowds came and he had many purchasers. The prices for most of the pictures were high, and so Richard would paint little cloud sketches in the evening and sell them the next day. He made over a thousand dollars. We all hoped he would use it for study; I had plans for Paris, but the money went where his affection dictated. He spent it on a sister who, he used to tell me, was more talented than he, in a vain attempt to cure her of what proved to be an incurable disease.

For a year he studied in Boston, living at the Robert Gould Shaw House; later he made beautiful posters of Du Bois's pageant. He went South. Before he left he came to see me at my studio. He talked more seriously than I had ever remembered before, though he was always a serious boy. I suppose I should not call him a boy since he was in his twenties, but his small stature and modest, quiet ways made him seem young. He wanted me to know that he loved his art as much as ever, but he could not paint as he used to because life was becoming so interesting to him. In West Virginia he only loved landscape. Now he watched faces, saw the bright girls as they went to high school, their books under their arms, interested, alert. Saw them deteriorate, their ambition lost as they saw no chance for advancement. He watched the great procession of Harlem and wanted to be able someday to paint it. "Not that I have forgotten what I want to do most of all. Someday, when I am the artist I hope to be, I want to return and paint those West Virginia hills."

We lingered a little to say good-bye. I can see the western sun flooding the room and then leaving us in a soft twilight. "You won't lose faith in me," he asked, "even though I do not produce anything for a time?" I told him I would never lose faith. And with that he went away, and I never saw him again. Like his sister, he died of an incurable disease.

Sometimes, when I look at the little landscape that he gave me, I wonder whether, had he lived, he could ever again have painted with such rare fidelity and such spiritual insight his West Virginia hills.

17 December 1932

In London at the Races' Congress

$\mathcal{I}$n July 1911 the First International Congress of Races was held in London. It had committees, honorary and executive, whose names fill thirty pages of its printed report. The prime minister of England, presidents of parliaments of the countries of the world, more Right Honorables than one knew existed, scientists, men of affairs, sociologists, writers, all endorsed the gathering.

Like everything else worthwhile, it was the product of a few minds. The secretary of the Ethical Culture Society, London, G. Spiller, was its executive secretary, with Felix Adler cooperating in New York. John E. Milholland, who lived much of his time in London, was the prime mover. Dr. Du Bois was the secretary of the American section. Quite a few Americans were present.

I crossed with Frances Bartholemew of Philadelphia, whose settlement work at 922 Locust Street had the most dramatic setting of any in the North. If Miss Bartholemew could be induced to write her reminiscences, she would have a story that would make mine commonplace. While a good settlement worker, she was a very bad sailor and we were both glad to see English soil.

It was disappointing soil, though. I had been reciting at intervals, as we steamed up the Channel, Arthur Hugh Clough's lovely poem "Green Fields of England" but found, when we landed and took the train, that the fields were parched and brown. Never had England known a worse drought. London was hot and sticky, and Hyde Park looked as parched as Central Park in August, only not so disreputable. New York, alone of the great cities of the world, allows its park to be used as a scrap basket.

The meetings of the Congress were at the University of London, whose metal roof heated us like a furnace. Of course, all our London acquaintances assured us that they had never known such heat before. They certainly were unprepared for it. The usual luncheon of cold meats and thick bread was everywhere served. Ice water was a luxury like diamonds. Few of us could attend the Conference all day under that hot roof.

I have the printed proceedings before me, a large volume filled with valuable information. Men exchanged papers before the Congress and to some extent answered one another. But the proceedings were different from the printed page. At first papers of some length were given. I remember Paul Reinsch, who felt that economic, literary, and social internationalism of today must make war impossible, and Felix von Luschan of Berlin, who believed that war would always exist and declared it was the enmity of Sparta that aroused the Athenians to national ardor and made them produce so great a civilization. But, as the Congress progressed, the speeches became shorter and shorter.

Of course, we were pressed for time, but also that Honorary Committee, with all its famous names, did not want anything said in criticism of imperialism. No complaints must be made.

Annie Besant defied this. She paced across the platform like a lioness, shaking her short hair as a lion might shake his mane. She said what she pleased and no one could stop her. But caution, and the heat, made the speeches run into platitudes and become boresome.

Only the Frenchman could make a little speech full of égalité and fraternité, saying nothing so charmingly that one listened entranced.

But if the speeches were not altogether a success, the social side of the Congress left nothing to be desired.

Think of a gathering of all the peoples of the world, some wearing their picturesque costumes—Hindoos, Chinese, Persians, Africans, West Indians, Egyptians, North American Indians, South Americans, all types of Europeans—the only people I remember not seeing were the Eskimos!

We were entertained in various ways. The Society of Fishmongers (what a lovely name) asked us to a reception in their majestic hall. I blush to think now of how I could not keep from playing the part of hostess—my settlement days were near then. The English pride themselves on never doing anything to bring people together, but what had we all taken this journey for but to meet? So, I moved about as if I were at home.

Jean Finot, whom I had already met, came over to me once

and said, "You seem to know all who are here. Could you maybe introduce me to the president of Haiti?"

I had M. Legitime pointed out and, of course, I made the introduction. They had a good time together.

But if the meeting at the Fishmongers' was successful it was eclipsed by the day when we were the guests of the Earl and Countess of Warwick at Warwick Castle. Our host and hostess were not with us, but that didn't matter. Their regrets were given by a representative who always spoke of "Warwick." Luncheon was served by liveried servants under the great cedars of Lebanon that were brought over during the Crusades. The informality of out-of-doors helped us to know one another.

The most beautiful person I saw was the daughter of the Haitian president, Mlle Legitime. She had been educated in Paris and spoke divine French. That's the right adjective to use. I am sure French is the language of heaven. Her face was dark, with finely moulded features, and her dark eyes were most expressive. But her grace especially impressed me. She picked up a peacock feather as she walked across the lawn and held it upright in her hand. (At the Spingarns in Amenia, the Lady of the Garden once picked a gladiolus for me and held it in the same way, but those are the only times I have seen such grace.)

I wished that all the Southern men who were then writing vituperously of the Negro might have been at Warwick Castle and have seen Mlle Legitime. They must immediately have lost their hearts to her, and, while they were struggling between love and pride, I would have had her turn her back on them and walk out of the picture. She and her father started me in my interest in Haiti, and I hope someday I may see that land of French culture and African hospitality before America has spoiled it.

Dr. Charles Alexander Eastman, North American Indian, was of our immediate party and with him we went away from the crowd to a knoll of trees of unusual beauty. "My people worship trees," he said and spoke of his tribe. Except that his color was a little too red, he looked to me like a perfectly good Yankee.

We went back from the knoll to mingle with this pageant of the nations, the Chinese, reticent, never looking at a woman since to do so in their land would be insulting; the Persians; the Hindoo in turban, a glutton for talk; the West Africans, able to outdo the Hindoos in volubility; Europeans. We moved over the noble estate and felt how deep down the roots went. And had we been in China or India or Egypt or Madagascar how much deeper still the roots would have gone. Here in America we are on the surface.

Our last meeting, an evening dinner, ended in some trouble that I did not understand, but I gathered that Milholland wanted a permanent organization with force to it, and the people in charge thought it best to disband. Certainly, we never had such a meeting again. The Pan African Congresses have been confined to one group of darker people. Any congresses of this sort are likely to come to grief, since in their very essence they are anti-imperialistic. They prove the equality of races, and the great nations are still engaged in refuting this doctrine. How often we hear that "these people are not yet ready for self-government."

London was then quite without race prejudice. Dr. W. A. Sinclair was one of the delegates to the Congress and he told me that he was almost embarrassed at the attention he received. People were anxious to have him know that they had no color prejudice. Still, then as now, a Southerner might make trouble for a colored boarder in pension or hotel.

Frances Bartholemew and I parted company shortly after the conference and I went with one of my oldest friends, Frances Davenport, now deceased, to Scandinavia. Frances Davenport was an historian working in the Carnegie Institution, a very painstaking, careful student. We had been in college together and loved to discuss the problems of the world.

One morning, about a month after the Races' Congress, we were sitting in a little park in Bergen, Norway, and got on the subject of war. I argued that the great wars were over. After our wonderful gathering, in which internationalism had been so much stressed, I felt this deeply. The world was becoming more and more a unit. Capitalism was international, and so were spiritual values. A famine in China brought instant aid from the United States. Ideas were international and inventions. And, above all, labor was becoming international.

My companion, who knew her facts, assured me that I was living in a dream world. That competition between European countries was never keener than at present. That, when the people in power wanted war, it would come.

I was in Paris that autumn of 1911 and saw a working-class demonstration at, I think, La Vilette. Germany and France were threatening war because of the Moroccan situation. The imperialists were militant, but the workers united for peace. The meeting I saw was one of a number. Guarded by mounted police, forbidden to march, the workers—syndicalists and socialists—made their speeches and sang the "Internationale." They were in a park, and outside, where the mounted police stayed, the old women jeered at authority from their windows. No one could have heard that singing and have seen the hatred on those women's faces and not have felt the power of the working class.

I suspect that those years directly before the Great War were the happiest before or since for the social worker. I know they were for me. Human ideas were common and with them one saw the beginning of wisdom. There was good work being done, and best of all there was hope. When at the Intercollegiate Socialist Society, just as at the gathering in Paris, we sang revolutionary songs, we felt our power. The workers were marching on, as William Morris said in his great hymn. The power of the despot, not only politically but economically, was breaking.

Well, we were oversanguine, but surely we were not such fools as the ruling class that started the war in 1914. Could they bring that summer back again, they would decide differently. They would make it up among themselves rather than start a world cataclysm.

24 December 1932

War

To those of us who were working for the Negro's full status as a citizen, the period directly before the World War held little encouragement. Just when one thought that the public was becoming educated, was learning to regard the Negro with some degree of justice, some frightful lynching would occur or some especially heinous example of legal justice would come to the NAACP office.

This happened in the Virginia Christian case, brought to our attention by the National Association of Colored Women. Virginia Christian, a girl of not more than sixteen years, had killed her mistress. She had a violent temper; the white woman had struck her, and she had rammed a towel down her tyrant's throat. She was convicted and sentenced to death. Miss Nerney, our secretary, went to Richmond and worked hard to secure clemency but without success. Virginia was hanged. The only white person who seemed at all concerned and really anxious to help the child was a Catholic priest. We gave the fullest publicity to the matter, and the State Farm for Colored Girls at Peak's Turnout was a result of this severe sentence.

Miss Janie Porter Barrett was placed at the head of the institution, and for years the colored women supported it, raising all the money. At length the State took it over and it is now a grade A institution, one of the best reformatories in the United States, and, while many of our prisons are unspeakable, our reformatories, or state farms, as they are more kindly named, rank high.

After the Virginia Christian case our NAACP office learned that *Birth of a Nation,* a dramatization of Dixon's *Clansman,* was to be produced as a moving picture by D. W. Griffith. We tried our best to get it censored but failed. It was produced in New York and at once proved a success. It told the story of Reconstruction to the glory of the Southern white and depicted the educated Negro as lusting after the white Southern girl. There were two beautiful white maidens; one was captured by the educated Negro and rescued by the noble band of Ku Klux; the other, a young and even more beautiful girl, was pursued by a loathsome black man, of the lowest criminal type, a man whose clawing hands appeared on the screen again and again. To escape from him she threw herself over a cliff and was found dead at its base.

New York gave the picture in its entirety. I was at the second production and watched the audience as much as the screen. The people were lapping it up. Many children were present and if they thought anything—they probably didn't; it wasn't a picture to arouse thought, but emotion—and if they did happen to remember their history, they must have despised Lincoln and Congress for freeing the slave. There were two old servants, very like baboons, who showed how much better the black man was before the North meddled with him. All the white Southern men, in the Ku Klux flowing sheets, were Sir Galahads.

We at the NAACP tried to do two things: to have the production stopped by our branches in the various towns where it was to be produced and to produce another film that should show a different side to the picture. We wholly failed in the second attempt. A well-known scenario writer made a film that would have been both interesting and reasonably favorable to the Negro, but it could not be produced without money to back it, and we had no money. The effort to have the branches stop the production, however, went on as long as *Birth of a Nation* lasted and was more than once crowned with success. It is remarkable how much power a few people in a community can exercise if they only put up a bold front. The Ohio Negroes have it to their lasting credit that the picture was not produced in their state.

I went to a hearing in Boston before Mayor Curley. The picture was due the following week and I had seen it in New York. The mayor was very much the good fellow, but he wanted me to remember that he was a Bostonian and that Boston was still the Athens of America. "You thought the picture terrible?" "Yes." "Did you think it as terrible as the murder of Duncan in Macbeth?" "Yes, more terrible than that." "Had I seen Richelieu?" "Yes." "Was it as bad as that?" "Yes, worse than that." I expected Othello to come next, but the mayor had perhaps exhausted his Shakespearean reading.

He told us that he couldn't prevent the production, though he could censor any portion dangerous to the morals of the people. "I stopped something the other day," he said, "because anyone could see how outrageous it was." This was the barefoot dancing of Isadora Duncan! But *Birth of a Nation*, with the pursuit scene cut out, showed its face on Beacon Hill.

Mr. Storey was at the hearing and also Griffith, the producer. When the meeting adjourned, Mr. Griffith went up to our NAACP president, who once was secretary to Charles Sumner, and held out his hand. "I am glad of the opportunity of meeting you, Mr. Storey," he said. Mr. Storey did not take the proffered hand. "I do not see why I should shake hands with you, Mr. Griffith," he answered in a voice that was quiet but severe.

I have an idea Griffith was the most surprised person at that moment in the United States. He was fine looking, had spoken eloquently, and looked as though he expected admiration, especially in the North. But he found the spirit of Sumner still in Boston. Mrs. Butler Wilson's eyes were filled with tears. "It was wonderful, Mr. Storey," she gasped. "It was wonderful of you." And, indeed, it was wonderful, for only a great conviction could have led so courteous a man to such an act.

I was in New York, working at what I supposed were important things, going from my home to my studio, to New York, home again, when of a sudden Europe went to war. The world changed overnight. Values were shifted, destroyed, and a sense of value is perhaps the most important thing we learn in life. I had worked to teach people to look with kindness at one another, to respect one another. I believed in the universality of culture. Among the essayists I cared most for was Matthew Arnold with his gospel of "Sweet Reasonableness." In the work that I had done, both among white and colored, I had tried to build up an environment that should bring people together, not separate them. The war shattered such work and such idealism as completely as it shattered the library at Louvain.

I joined the pacifists because I had not the slightest use for the cause for which either side fought. I liked Germany better than any other European country—my father had a few business friends there, and he loved it dearly—and I couldn't see, with England's record in Ireland and India, why she should be considered less imperialistic than her neighbor. They seemed to me all tarred with the same brush and when America entered it was just the same.

Had ours been a war to end some form of slavery, like the Civil War, I doubt whether my pacifism would have held. But the name showed that I hated war, and that was true enough. One can't draw fine lines in times of great emotional appeal. And as the days and weeks and months went on, and one awoke every morning, first to the happiness of the sun streaming through the window, a second later to the recollection of youth killing youth, and worse, maiming, blinding, crippling it, of starving children, of burning homes, of lovely forests cut down to give place to barbed wire, of noise and vermin and lechery, it was scarcely possible to glorify the conflict. Rather, it seemed difficult to remain sane.

Of course, I should have also seen courage, heroism, the love of one comrade for another. But I didn't. War today may be tactically interesting. But it reads like a chemical laboratory. The spear that Achilles hurled at Hector had become a bomb of gas, that, if it does not kill, leaves a wound far more horrible than any the Trojans bore. No, as I read the papers, there was nothing inspiring in the battle.

One thing gradually became evident, especially after we entered the war. Not those who started the conflict but the darker peoples of Asia and Africa, and even the Negro in America, might benefit by it. A war brings a nation together in common defense.

When we had entered the war Negroes and whites were alike needed as soldiers, and in the drives for money Negro money brought supplies just the same as white. So, while there were an infinite number of petty insults, of annoying incidents, the Negro did become a part of the country as he had not been before. I remember a colored woman, at Des Moines, who drove me in her car. It bore a Red Cross seal, and whites made way for her, because of what she represented.

We found plenty of work to do at the NAACP. Our chairman, Mr. J. E. Spingarn, soon to be Major Spingarn, before entering the army, worked and succeeded in getting a training camp for colored soldiers. He was convinced, and we can see that he was right, that the Negro would never get to be a commissioned officer if he relied for his training on getting into white officers' camps. After entrance in the army, Major Spingarn worked in the military intelligence department until he was sent overseas. Our secretary, Roy Nash, enlisted and became a captain in the artillery. Dr. Du Bois was sent by the association to France to investigate discrimination among the colored soldiers. The head of our legal committee, Mr. Arthur B. Spingarn, became Captain Spingarn in the surgeon general's division. I was one of the few volunteers left in the office and I was glad to find a perfectly good reason for withdrawing from Liberty Loan and Y drives. Hardly a week passed in which the National office did not receive some complaint regarding the treatment of colored soldiers, or their status, in the various camps. Somebody must be on that job.

Among the many cases of injustice and discrimination, none angered me as much as the treatment of Colonel Charles Young.

I first met Colonel Young in Boston when he was presented with the Spingarn medal. It was a frightfully stormy night, and, fortunately for me, I had gone to the city the day before. The presentation was to be preceded by a small dinner at the Hotel Bellevue, and when I entered the dining room I was greeted with enthusiasm and relief. The secretary, Roy Nash, and other New York guests had not arrived and the report from the railroad station gave little hope that a train could get through for some hours. So, the honors that would have been divided all came to me, and I sat between Colonel Young and Moorfield Storey.

Charles Young was a strikingly handsome man of magnificent physique and with a dark, mobile face. I was with him later at a dinner at the Henry Street Settlement when we were at war and he was in uniform. The half-dozen newly created soldiers present could not keep away from this superior officer, so impressive in his quiet simplicity. We had a very good time at the Boston dinner and I hated to leave the hotel and attend the meeting. One does get tired of both hearing and making speeches. But the meeting held a surprise, for Colonel Young made a memorable speech. He was the second of our medalists, Ernest Just having set an example of a simple murmured thank-you when the medal was given.

Colonel Young said not a word of criticism of his treatment in the service of his country, but somehow one felt that he had suffered much. When the war came and he was denied the right to lead Negro troops, he still said no word of complaint. The excuse was that he was ill, had a high blood pressure, kidney trouble. As though this would have mattered had he been wanted! And when at length his orders came to move to Africa, he also said no word of complaint, but he knew, and his wife knew, that, in going to Liberia again, he was going to his death.

Well, it's all over now, but among the martyrs of the Negro race I count Colonel Charles Young.

We lived through the war, and, when it was all over and the

countries looked into their affairs, there was a chance for irony. The Kaiser and the Tsar, two of the leading conspirators, were, one in exile, the other dead. The victors were enormously in debt and were soon to find that the imperialism for which they had fought was less secure than when they began. Europe had battled to control Asia and Africa and had come out the worse for her pains. The American Negro, to whom no one had given a thought, found himself better off than he had ever been before. Foreign immigration had stopped and he was getting new jobs. The returning soldiers, some fifty thousand of them, had gained in experience and in self-respect. South was moving North and North was learning the feel of good money.

I remember the first time I dared to ask for five- and ten-dollar memberships. It was in New Bedford and the money came, one bill swiftly after another. "You mustn't let Mr. Pickens get ahead of me," I said (Mr. Pickens had lately come to our staff), and one of the men, middle-aged, a sturdy workman who had given ten dollars, said to me afterward, "We didn't let you down, did we?" I raised about two hundred dollars in that night, an unheard-of sum for a small town. Discrimination might be rampant, but there was something to fight with; there was courage, hope, and money.

In January 1919, the board of the NAACP elected me its chairman. I had been acting chairman since 1917. Mr. Spingarn, who had given us the inestimable value of his name, felt that he could not retain the office any longer; he would be absent from New York for long periods. So, I was promoted to chairman. It was like the boy in the storybook, "from errand boy to president." I need not say that the promotion was gratifying to me.

31 December 1932

How Texas Mobbed John R. Shillady

$\mathcal{I}$n 1918, at Mr. Villard's insistence, the NAACP decided to employ as secretary a man trained to executive work and with years of success behind him. The person chosen was John R. Shillady, the executive force behind the famous work of Everit V. Macy in Westchester County.

Mr. Shillady had graying hair, but a youthful face, tall, broad-shouldered, a pleasing personality. He at once showed his driving power. Branch membership in a year grew from nine thousand to forty-four thousand paid-up members. Our office staff increased. We moved into larger quarters at 70 Fifth Avenue. And during Mr. Shillady's leadership we had the enormously successful Cleveland Conference [and] the two-day Conference against Lynching, in New York at the Bar Association Building, Moorfield Storey presiding. We became a great national organization with recognized power. It was the building up of a body of supporters all over the country that made our work of the past ten years possible.

The work had been well begun by the man who was in Mr. Shillady's time our field secretary, James Weldon Johnson, but, with a well-organized office running on the most modern methods back home, Mr. Johnson's work became less difficult. We had been disorganized for a time with the loss of Roy Nash. Now we were to become a firmly knit, well-appointed national organization.

I had been acting chairman before Mr. Shillady came and had represented the association at various functions. The month after the new secretary's installation, I was invited with him to a dinner of the Urban League. He was the one asked to speak. I had been doing the speech making, and for the moment I felt left out.

Then I saw a small table by a window with two seats, at one of which sat a tall, elderly gentleman wearing a high, old-fashioned collar. I asked whether I might join him and, when he assented, sat down to the most pleasant dinner of the year. For my neighbor

88

opposite was Mr. John E. Nail, an old time New Yorker, who knew his New York as Dickens knew his London. He might have been Tim Linkinwater for his enthusiasm over the city's streets. I also am the city's child and could boast that my grandfather met Robert Fulton and later had been praised as a bright lad by Albert Gallatin. Also, that my great-grandfather had built a factory on Houston Street that was dubbed "Ovington's Folly" because it was the immense height of four stories.

When I looked at Mr. Shillady, squeezed in, at the speakers' table, his broad shoulders bumping his neighbors, I lost all envy. It was good to have what proved to be one of many talks with so congenial a companion, and, while near the crowd, not to be of it.

But this was one example that made me realize my work as chairman would be largely advisory. I didn't like that. I had worked at the office so long, doing everything from stamping letters to receiving distinguished guests, that the love of the place had grown on me. I wanted a settled task, and, looking around, I found one that no one else had the time to fill. We had a field secretary but no branch secretary to take charge of the work at the office. So, with Mr. Shillady's approval, I added the position of branch secretary to that of chairman and for over a year went to the office daily and heartily enjoyed the branch work.

I took over branch correspondence, edited the *Branch Bulletin*, and, with Mr. Harry E. Davis at the other end, handled the Cleveland conference.

Mr. Shillady arranged an anti-lynching conference culminating in a meeting, at which two great celebrities, Charles Evans Hughes and Anna Howard Shaw, spoke. We had friendly rivalry regarding our conferences, and, if his surpassed in luminaries' mine was longer and gave more people a chance to speak!

As always, the most important part of our yearly gathering is the coming together of people from all over the country, and the comparing of notes over the luncheon table or at dinner in some pleasant home.

It was at Cleveland that I grew to know the Chesnutts, and Helen Chesnutt lent me her country cottage after the conference was over. I had a week between Cleveland and a meeting of the National Federation of Colored Women's Clubs at Zanesville, Ohio, and I didn't want to go back to New York. Miss Chesnutt's hospitality, the quiet, restful week alone in her little place among the foothills, led me later to buy a place in the country myself.

I wish I could make my readers realize the tremendous courage and enthusiasm that all we NAACP workers felt after our two conferences were over, the one in New York on lynching, in May, the other, the national conference, in Cleveland the end of June. Thanks to our new publicity director, Herbert J. Seligman, the newspapers had found us out and had given us plenty of space. Especially Mr. Shillady had reason to be encouraged, since Hughes had spoken at Carnegie Hall against lynching. Our volume on *Thirty Years of Lynching in the United States,* which Martha Gruening had compiled and which had been lying around unfinished for some time for lack of funds, was now brought into shape by Frank Morton and published. It has furnished facts to all the world and is the basis for all American lynching statistics. James Weldon Johnson and Walter White, by their careful, and often dangerous, investigations of current lynchings, had at last broken down the country's indifference. Our organization was like a boy who has been growing from babyhood through childhood to youth, but is gawky, loose-limbed. Then suddenly, almost overnight, the youth becomes a man.

In early August, when, after our two conferences, we were resting a little, as victors rest after they have demonstrated their strength, we received a disquieting letter from our branch at Austin, Texas. It seemed that their books had been called for by the Attorney General and their affairs looked into. The branch had shown its sympathy with the Negroes sent to jail at Austin for complicity in the Longview, Texas, riots.

The story of Longview should be written up someday, but it does not belong here. Unquestionably, it was a symbol of that unrest that was pervading the South after the Negro soldiers came back from the war. The white South feared them not so much because of immediate rioting, but because they distrusted their willingness to accept the position of inferiority that their states had always demanded. They might try to vote, to oppose segregation in jim crow cars, in court, to stand for the things the NAACP stood for. The Austin branch sold the *Crisis* magazine, but all the colored newspapers published the resolutions of the Cleveland conference, in which segregation on public carriers was condemned. White officials at Austin had seen this statement and the branch was called to account.

Now Texas was one of our strongholds. It had twenty-nine

branches, two of them, Dallas and San Antonio, with paid-up memberships of one thousand and of fifteen hundred. If Austin closed down, the movement might spread throughout the state. We never sanctioned violence, and our work against segregation was mapped out upon national, not state, lines. Once understood, I felt that opposition would subside, and I asked Mr. Shillady whether he would go to Texas and present our association to the Attorney General and the Governor.

I recall how we stood in his office talking the matter over. When I said that I believed he was the man to win over the Texas officials, he asked me quietly whether I thought there would be danger. I looked at him as he stood there, a gentleman, not only in speech and manner, but in instinct, and I pictured him as meeting other gentlemen, officers of the state. "There might be danger to someone else," I said, "but not to you." And with that we went on to plans of just when he should go and the literature to be sent ahead of him.

Many of my readers remember what happened. Mr. Shillady reached Austin in the evening and the next day went to the statehouse. The Governor was away; so was the Attorney General. He saw the acting Attorney General and explained our work and its legal character. The acting Attorney talked about "niggers" and the danger of letting them think they could break down segregation. "You may be thinking in the future," he said, "but the niggers will expect to get these things right now."

The talk shifted to lynching and Mr. Shillady showed the "Address to the Nation" which had been published in connection with the Anti-Lynching Conference, which was signed by many persons of national prominence. He assured the Attorney General that no association which had secured the signatures to an appeal against mob violence of such eminent men as the Attorney General of the United States and the governors of several states could have any connection with organizing Negroes to put down the whites. He was dismissed in a courteous manner and started to call upon the captain of the state Rangers.

But before he had walked any distance he was touched on the arm by a constable, served with a subpoena, and haled before a secret session of what was called a "court of inquiry." Here the tone was hostile. They must have been a tough-looking lot who took part in the meeting. Only the stenographer, a young girl, showed any sympathy, and she, of course, could not express it. The NAACP in its resolutions at the Cleveland conference was accused of attempting to violate the laws of Texas by favoring abolishing the jim crow car. Mr. Shillady answered that the resolution applied to proposed action by the federal Congress. The usual type of thread-worn questions was asked, as, "Would you want your daughter to marry a nigger?" "Why don't you stop at a nigger hotel?" Mr. Shillady wrote into the record the names he had mentioned to the Attorney General, prominent men supporting us, calling attention to two Texas names.

He was dismissed at last and should not have ventured out the next day until he went to his train. But John R. Shillady was not a man to shirk any responsibility he had undertaken. Consequently, the following morning he visited an officer of the branch and, on his return to his hotel, was again tapped on the arm. He thought a second subpoena was being served and made no attempt to defend himself, when he was struck in the face, was surrounded by men, among them County Judge Dave Pickle, who had been at the evening's hearing, and, after being showered with blows, was left almost unconscious.

When he entered the hotel, the clerk said, "I wouldn't have your job for a thousand dollars." He telephoned the mayor for police protection and got to the depot and into the train without further assault, though a menacing crowd was gathered in the railroad station. Then he had a long railroad ride, over twenty-four hours in the state of Texas alone, before he should reach home.

We at the office were finishing an afternoon's work when someone who was reading the evening paper called out that Mr. Shillady had been attacked in Austin. Of course, we all felt alarmed and we didn't get word directly from him until twenty-four hours had passed. His wife was frantic. At length his train came into the station. Every red cap who could possibly get away rushed to meet it. It was a triumphant procession to the office.

I sent a telegram as chairman of the board to the governor of Texas, W. P. Hobby, describing the treatment given our representative and asking what efforts were being made to punish the offenders. The governor replied that Shillady was the only offender and that he had been punished before our inquiry came. That was the reply not only of the governor but of the people of Austin. We tried to get in touch with some liberal sentiment but could find none.

I know that I am severe upon the South. I feel it as I write these reminiscences. But it is not because they do such terrible things; it is because they extenuate these things. The city of New York today is one of the worst-governed cities of the world. I, as a New Yorker, acknowledge it. But not a person in Austin would acknowledge that it was wrong to beat up a visitor who had come to the city to make a courteous inquiry into the reasons for suspending the work of the organization he represented. I suppose the law-abiding people were terrorized, just as thousands of our business-men today are terrorized by racketeers. Again, we in New York have nothing to boast of. But I have never heard the racketeer praised for his violence by the governor of New York.

The Southerner not only excuses the present, he still excuses, extenuates, the past. He writes American history, and our youth is taught that the Negro was always worthless when given power, that the abolitionist was a fool and that on the whole slavery was beneficent.

When the Southerner is as ashamed of slavery as the New Englander is of the slave trade, when he despises the slave block and the plantation system that made it profitable as much as the New Englander despises the slave ship, then he will have a new South to reveal to us. For the South, like the North, had its heroic protesters against slavery, its men like Helper of North Carolina, its women like the Grimké sisters. There were great spirits in the mountains and even in the bottom lands, and, when history is written from the workers' standpoint, their names will shine more brightly than Jefferson's or Lee's.

Mr. Shillady left the NAACP the following spring. We wanted to have a great case down in Austin and every lawyer in the association would have liked to help it. But his wife looked upon the matter personally and did not intend that we should use her husband for the purpose of exploiting our organization. He had done enough.

But we made a gesture of defiance by holding our next conference in Atlanta, Georgia. Instead of six, we arranged for three days of meetings so that we could get away early. But Atlanta treated us royally, and there were white men, the late Plato Durham I remember especially, who attended our sessions every evening. The press gave us unusually fine publicity, featuring on its front page our demands for unsegregated traveling accommodations and for the vote. So, I end this chapter with a good word for the South, after all.

7 January 1933

National Association of Colored Women

$\mathcal{I}$ have written of my work at the NAACP as Branch Director. It led to my speaking before a number of branches, but I did not go far afield until 1920. That year I was invited to attend the annual conference of the National Association of Colored Women (NACW) at Denver, Colorado. If I went, my expenses would have to be paid by our Association, so it was arranged that I should do a considerable amount of Branch work on my way to Denver and on my return.

I felt quite professional starting out, not only with the usual suitcase, but also with a briefcase and a typewriter. My first stop was at Pittsburgh, and I marveled how a Branch could survive that had such hills to climb. Not as many people owned cars then as now and this Alpine work took up time. There was nothing Alpine-like in the welcome given me, however. Everyone was most cordial. I remember especially the women who were working for us, among them Mrs. Daisy Lampkin, who is now one of our field secretaries. Pittsburgh's grime was there, but not much worse than New York's.

The next branch visited was Peoria, Illinois, a name then associated with jokes about whiskey. I don't know what I expected, but I was surprised to find an attractive city with a lovely parkway. Our late afternoon drive will always remain in my memory. The branch president, Mrs. B. H. West, planned and executed a royal welcome. And, from then on, I tasted the West's hospitality.

I suppose the people who now rush across the continent in their motors, making four and even five hundred miles in twenty-four hours, think they know the country they go through. I am sure they don't. Pretty much the only views they have a chance to see are those from the filling stations. I moved in leisurely fashion, viewing the world from the car window and stopping at many cities on the way. Sometimes I went to a hotel, more often I was entertained in the home of one of the branch members.

At Moline I got out at the wrong station and came near missing a cordial welcome, both from my hostess and from the members of the branch who came to the station to meet me, finding me at last, on the streetcar.

I went to a modest home with pretty grounds about it and was given the best room in the house, my host and hostess moving out for me. I always know when this happens by the gay line of neckties strung against the wall. Other things are removed but never the neckties.

I had been North and South but never west of Chicago. This was just after the war and we were feeding the world. How impressive the Mississippi valley was with its unending fields of wheat and corn. I had seen corn in the South but not corn like this. The fertility was amazing to one whose country life had chiefly been in New England. In comparison, the New England fields seemed no larger than the minute valleys of Norway, where only one or two families can live. On and on we went, until it became incredible that anyone in the country should be hungry. And today people are starving and the grain is rotting! I read not long ago in a scientific article that man's reasoning power is, biologically, in its infancy, not nearly so old as man's emotions. One scarcely needs to have this pointed out.

We had a thriving branch at Omaha, where Father Williams was an active worker.

As usual, I took a walk in a park and saw a cowbird mothered by a thrush. This may not seem worth recording, but it is one of the amusing things in nature, something of which I had often read but had never seen before. The cowbird was almost as large as the thrush, entirely capable of taking care of itself but tagged after the mother that had hatched it and refused to be shaken off. The thrush, agitated, perplexed, scolding her best, yet continued her maternal duties, feeding a child that could have fed itself.

I had dinner that night with two charming colored girls from Canada, and in their bird book they corroborated my identification.

It so happens that I have many friends in the library world and I went to the public library at Omaha to meet one of them. As usual, I found her interested in my work. I think that the Negro does not see the library as a public center as much as he might. Librarians want to please their public and they always welcome the intelligent reader of books. The careful reader would be amazed to know how much careless reading there is, a book taken out, skimmed for a possible thrill, never finished. The demand for fiction in such excess of anything else is disheartening. When, therefore, a colored person comes to the library and asks what recent accessions there have been on the Negro or on race prejudice (two subjects one must be up on), it is a pleasure to the librarian to help him. Many librarians will put the *Crisis* on their shelves. More than the school, the library could be used to put the race problem before the country. For the more the Negroes take out good books, the more they will be bought.

At Kansas City, Missouri, and at Kansas City, Kansas, I found Mrs. Cook and Mrs. Dwiggan among the unforgettable women who have been loyal to the NAACP. They had many engagements for me to fill, and when I reached Denver I was ready to go to a hotel and rest before the National Association of Colored Women opened its session.

Resting, with me, included taking a walk. I thought I would start to find my way about the city and I walked to the Negro section and back. The altitude hit me on the head! The remainder of the day was spent resting, quite literally. I wish someone would explain why the altitude in the Rockies is more difficult to endure than the altitude in Switzerland.

Mrs. Mary Talbert was the president of the National at that time and opened the session with her usual dignity and sincerity. She was then engaged in the prodigious and successful work of saving the Frederick Douglass home. I had the honor of knowing Mrs. Talbert and of visiting her at Buffalo in her old-fashioned home, and I want to pay my tribute to one of the most intelligent workers with whom I have ever cooperated. She worked untiringly for the NACW. She worked for the NAACP investigating jim crow conditions in Texas, starting branches, and encouraging those already existing. When James Weldon Johnson became secretary, she organized a woman's auxiliary that made possible his great work against lynching.

The women turned in, not hundreds, but thousands of dollars. They made possible our spectacular page in the *New York Times* headed "The Shame of America." They aroused their public to give us money. Mrs. Talbert worked to her physical limit. But her spirit refused to recognize this limit and she ended her life through zeal for service.

My readers know a great deal more about the National Association of Colored Women than I do. Some know it from the inside with its discouragements and jealousies. I saw it at its best, but, making all allowance for the optimism of reports, I was profoundly moved by the character and amount of work done. My impressions, as a white woman conversant with social work, may be of interest.

Two existing women's organizations formed the NACW, one of them, the National Federation of Colored Women's Clubs. Perhaps because this was a New England movement, the National Federation was the name in my mind when I went to Denver and I expected to meet with women's clubs somewhat similar to the clubs among whites with which I was familiar.

My mother joined the Brooklyn Woman's Club when I started, and when only one other woman's club could claim priority, Sorosis, of New York. These clubs were frankly cultural. Women had few opportunities then for education and the club was intended to keep up their reading and study, to give them something beside the daily household round. My generation, that had more opportunity for education, looked down on these clubs and made fun of the papers that discussed Roman history in half an hour or covered the field of painting in one session. Clubs like this, I do not doubt, were in the National Federation of New England and in Washington and other cities. But the National Association of Colored Women, as I met with it, was not working along cultural lines but along social service lines. It was starting kindergartens and day nurseries and looking after old people. And it was raising money, in nickels and dimes and quarters, but to an astonishing amount. I never saw anything like it before, and I have never seen anything like it since.

Their motto was "Lifting as We Climb." Not kicking down the ladder as soon as a slight social eminence was reached, but helping up the one below. The work was given its first impetus nearly thirty years ago by a white physician who wrote an insulting article in which he made the statement that there was not a chaste colored woman in the United States over sixteen.

Some Negro club women met, drew up a strong statement to the country, and then all came together determined to begin service for those young girls of whom this indictment was true. They met at Washington. Frederick Douglass was there. Among the many prominent women was Mrs. Ruffin of Boston; Mrs. Hunton, then a young bride; and, of course, one who has always fought for colored women, Mary Church Terrell. Mrs. Terrell was elected the first president of the National Association of Colored Women.

I listened at Denver to the reports from all sections of the country. In the North, the National's work supplemented the work of organizing charity and of the city and state. In the South, the Negro had to do pretty much everything. What money the city or county or state appropriated for the poor, the sick, the delinquent, was appropriated for the white. Only the courts were busy with the Negro, sending the young boy to the chain gang, the girl to execution, as in the case already mentioned of Virginia Christian. So, the Negro women went to work and out of their scanty means provided old people's homes, opened day nurseries, started work among delinquents.

As I sat and listened, I was thankful that the NAACP existed, pounding away as it did on the issue of full citizenship. But I was glad that the women were doing what they could before these rights were won. Their accomplishments were many. Their work was not always up to the standard, but they had little money and must do the best with that they had. They were all volunteers, and the desire for position, the only reward that can be given a volunteer, was obvious. The greatest menace, common in all volunteer organizations, was the tendency of some workers to grow inactive after the positions they desired were won. But by and large they were hard workers, generous givers.

I wish their story might be written someday and given to the world. Negro work built up by some individual has been frequently featured. Individual Negroes have been honored, but the white world, and white women especially, have no appreciation of the amount of social service work that colored women, without wealth or leisure, have accomplished.

I made my little speech at Denver and was warmly received. I left, grateful for this opportunity. I went as far north as St. Paul and Minneapolis on my return trip, and, when at length I sat down at my desk, I felt that the *New Yorker* was provincial as well as Sinclair Lewis's hero of *Main Street*. There still is diversity in this country if we want to find it. But who wants diversity, anyway? Many are the Americans who ask for fried eggs and cornbeef hash at a Paris restaurant.

14 January 1933

The Stage

For my future happiness in life, I was fortunate in being brought up by people who loved the stage and liked a good play even more than a good book. Their taste was discriminating and I saw many of the great tragedians, Edwin Booth, Lawrence Barrett, Henry Irving, Ellen Terry, Modjeska. *Macbeth*, with Booth and Modjeska, was the greatest theatrical production I have ever seen or am likely to see. I saw comedies of a high order, Sheridan and Goldsmith, and, among modern material, adaptations of German farces at Daley's. The actors and actresses were thoroughly at home on the stage, not only in their movements but in their speech, for they believed that the proper use of the speaking voice was as important as the acting. I never heard today's mumbling or the rasping voice, like a grating file, of that otherwise delightful actor, Alfred Lunt.

We all acted at home, and I appeared on the boards at three as the Fairy Cricket on the Hearth. We children dramatized our storybooks and were especially strong in Dickens's scenes. But my father was the only one with real talent. I am confident he could have moved Broadway audiences as he did the intimate ones in our parlor, where, with the slightest attempt at scenery and with old-fashioned footlights, he brought complete illusion and sent men's hearts to their throats. I used to sit in a child's rocker in the front of the first row and wonder how so quiet a man could suddenly change and show every emotion from great joy to despair.

Musical comedy was gay with Gilbert and Sullivan's pleasant satire. Lillian Russell and Frank Wilson were at the Casino. Klaw and Erlanger were soon to give Drury Lane adaptations, that (little did I realize this) owed their lyrics to a man who was to become my friend at work and at play, in the city and in the country, James Weldon Johnson.

With this as a background, as soon as I became interested in the Negro, I went to see him on the stage. After the first performance, Cole and Johnson's *Shoo Fly Regiment,* I was a devotee and, whenever I got a chance, went to my first favorites and to Ernest Hogan, to Sam Dudley, and to those priceless comedians, Williams and Walker. I saw them all and read about them and took my friends to see them. It was such gay farce, but, back of it, as is true of sincere mirth, was a strain of sadness.

I can see Ernest Hogan, at the end of a first act (was it *The Oysterman*?), his great eyes shining, his face puzzled, suspecting deceit, but too simple-minded to be able to fathom how he is being duped. Sam Dudley, poor, ragged, only his mule for company, dreams outside the White House gates that he will shave the president. Even when one howled over Williams's song of "Nobody," one felt a queer tenderness for the big man.

These shows were written for Negro audiences and, except in New York, were played chiefly to Negro audiences. With the death of one after another of the leading actors and the seizure by the moving picture of the modest theaters which these shows could rent, they went out of existence. Later, Miller and Lyles, in *Shuffle Along,* revived the tradition and played to crowded audiences. But the old days were over and fashion took the Negro into new fields. The revue became popular, and new names, the late Florence Mills, Josephine Baker in Paris, Bill Robinson, and many others that I do not know shone in brilliant letters before theater entrances.

But the important place that the Negro was to occupy on the stage was not only to be measured by his success in musical comedy and revue. In 1917 three plays written by Ridgely Torrence were presented by a group of colored players at the Garden Theater. One was a comedy, *The Rider of Dreams;* one a tragedy, *Granee Maumee;* and one, *Simon the Cyrenian,* the story of a black man who was Jesus's crossbearer.

Ridgely Torrence is poet rather than playwright, and he was therefore fortunate in having his plays interpreted by a poetic race. The run was short, but everyone who went felt the beauty of the acting and the remarkable orchestration, led by Rosamond Johnson. Especially Opal Cooper made a name for himself in his part in *The Rider of Dreams.*

But it was three years later that New York learned the possibilities of the Negro tragedian. November 3, 1920, saw *The Emperor Jones* produced at the Provincetown Theater, with Charles Gilpin in the title role. America's greatest playwright had written a great Negro play and just the right man had been found to act the leading part.

Gilpin's acting brought fame to the Provincetown, to O'Neill, and to himself. He had been in small road shows before this until he was given a poor part in Drinkwater's *Lincoln,* a part which he made intelligent and beautiful. By chance he was cast for *The Emperor Jones* and the next morning acclaimed a great tragedian. He had carried through a piece in which he was practically the only actor, the story of a powerful man, harried by fear, haunted by the sorrows of his race, but towering above the cheap cockney and the timid workers. His splendid voice, his noble physique, his portrayal of, first, suspicion then self-confidence breaking down under fear, then repentance, last terror, left one breathless. Those of us who saw all this at that little barnlike theater, sitting on its wooden benches, like Austin Dobson in his famous rondeau:

> Thrilled with all changes of despair,
> Hope, anger, fear, desire and doubt,
> When Burbage played.

Most unforgettable was the vision of the slave ship, the figures huddled together, moaning. Irresistibly, Gilpin is drawn into this image of his past; he joins the huddled figures and when they moan his voice rises above theirs in a tragic cry. And, through all, the drum gives its inexorable beat.

Gilpin dominated the theater when playing *The Emperor Jones.* They tell an amusing story of how one night, when he was late in arriving, and director and manager and others were worried and hectic, the callboy, a smart little Italian who bossed them all, rushed up to Charles Cram, saying, "Keep your shirt on, Ginks," and, turning to Ida Rowe, "Quit fussin', Ida. It's all right. MR. GILPIN IS HERE."

With *The Emperor Jones*, plays using Negro material poured upon New York. The Provincetown produced *All God's Chillun Got Wings,* Paul Robeson in the leading part. O'Neill could not make his public care as much for this story of a Negro-white marriage as for his Emperor, but he did the theater-loving world a good turn by taking Robeson out of a lawyer's office and putting him where he belonged. *Deep River* came and, with it, Rose McClendon. After the premiere of that musical drama, the critics poured out praise of this new actress, a colored woman who, as Octavie, came down the staircase at the octoroon ball and gave her few lines with a compelling grace. In *Deep River* Bledsoe sang, his great voice at its best. Many short plays cropped up. Paul Green won the Pulitzer Prize with *In Abraham's Bosom*, partly because his chief character was taken by a new genius, Frank Wilson. Gilpin produced Nan Bagly Stephen's *Roseanne*, with Rose McClendon as leading lady. In New York it grew to be the custom to give a Negro part to a Negro, not to a blacked-up white man. Colored men and women gained wide experience on the stage, where formerly they had had very specialized roles. And then came the production of *Porgy* by New York's famous Theater Guild.

I went to see *Porgy* three times and only wished I could spend the money to go oftener. The first time I sat by two Southern men, evidently visitors to New York. Before the curtain rose they talked about "coons" and "niggers." At the end of the first scene they were bored. At the end of the second, the marvelous picture of the "Wake," they agreed that they had come to a good show. When they left they were convinced, terribly against their wills, but convinced, that the Negro was a great actor. My second performance was a matinee, and when the first act was over I noticed that my neighbor at my right was restless. After a minute or two she spoke. "I must talk to someone," she said. "Don't you think the play wonderful?" We engaged in exclamations of enthusiasm and then she told me that her sister had written a Negro pageant. "You see," she said, "I have always been interested in the Negro." The Atlanta University Pageant had recently been given in New York. "You don't happen to be Gertrude Ware's sister?" I asked. She was. It did seem extraordinary that, in that great audience, I should by chance have been sitting by a daughter of the founder of Atlanta University!

Porgy brought forward a number of new Negro actors, though none to equal Wilson and Rose McClendon. When its vogue was over its cast went home or secured other parts or went into the movies. Of course, there is another story of the moving picture successes of the Negro world, another of the concert hall, another of the radio. Musical and dramatic ability have always been associated with the race but, until recently, have only been allowed a small, humorous type of expression. But DuBose Heyward in *Porgy* gave his actors great parts, and once they had shown their ability they were cast elsewhere. The highest point, however, was not reached until Marc Connelly wrote and directed *The Green Pastures* and gave his morality play to the world.

There is much controversy concerning *The Green Pastures* among colored people, but none among whites. From its first night it was a pronounced success and its vogue has continued to today. Four things have contributed to this, first, the genius of Marc Connelly, who must have heard the eerie fairy tales of Ireland from some old grandmother, so full are his plays of delicate imagery, so little like the blatant Irish American. Second, Richard Harrison, whose portrayal of the Lawd amazes everyone by its simplicity, its homely likeness to the faithful Negro preacher, and yet its awful dignity and power. Third, Hall Johnson, who trained the chorus, bringing the spirituals to us as they are rarely sung today. And last, Robert Edmund Jones, whose scenery and costumes carry out unerringly the simple, poetic character of the story.

I saw *The Green Pastures* in rehearsal but cared more for it the second time, some months later. At the rehearsal I was wondering whether the play would get over, questioning this and that in my mind. I remember caring most for the little scene at the dining table, where Noah recognizes the Lawd. It is exquisite in its poetry, and there is none of the theatricalism of Haynes in Tutt Whitney's acting. In genius Whitney is a close second to Harrison. But at my second performance no one thing stood out. I saw the play as a whole, and I understood why people in the orchestra were as reverent as at a church service. The place was packed. I was in the last row, and the men and women standing back of me were as silent as they would have been at a Philharmonic concert. Mr. Harrison told me that priests sent their congregations to see the play in Lent and that nuns were sometimes in the audience. I believe *The Green Pastures* has made more converts than any evangelist who has been preaching since the play began.

With this opinion of the play, I have talked with colored people, friends and acquaintances, and have usually found myself in disagreement. Indeed, so much have we disagreed it seemed best to let the subject drop. But a writer has the chance to say her say without being answered back, and I cannot resist discussing this adverse attitude, for it explains many difficulties that the Negro artist has to meet.

The great success of *The Green Pastures*, Harrison's superb acting, the music of the chorus, has modified Negro criticism. Nothing succeeds like success. But the core of the play, its folk character, remains under suspicion. Negroes, they say, wouldn't conceive of fish frys and picnics in heaven. That is the most damning scene. But all of heaven is suspect except the last scene. The laughter of the audience can't be right. They are laughing at the Negro's doing silly things. Why do they always show the ignorant Negro? Why can't they show us at our best? This last plaintive criticism is heard at every successful colored show.

Can I answer this and make my point clear without being offensive? The reason, I am convinced, is that the Negro of *The Green Pastures* belongs to a social sphere that, though humble, is deep-rooted, while the educated Negro today has been uprooted and has rarely achieved a culture comparable artistically to the old. He is heroically trying to keep up with the procession, but, except as he is opposed in this by the white man, he is not a striking figure. And the artist chooses the striking figure. (Only the very great can illumine, as Jane Austen did, the commonplace in life.) As an example of what I mean: The son of a Maine fisherman comes to New York, buys a Hart, Schaffner, and Marx suit of clothes, gets a job in a shop, and feels that these city folk ought to know how he had advanced over his forebears. But does the artist notice him? Not at all, unless it be to make fun of him. Instead, he goes down to Maine, finds the father, who, in his oilskins, has come back from a morning's catch, hears salty talk and stories of adventure and hardships as old as the sea itself. Here is reality, a culture that is secure. So, Marc Connelly's folk go back, not to Maine but to the Green Pastures of Louisiana, and give us something secure, deep-rooted, imaginative as the heart of a child.

I have spoken of the one time that the educated Negro is a dramatic figure, the time when he is opposed in his ambition by the white man. The Provincetown Theater, always interested in new powerful drama, recently produced a play on this theme, Annie Nathan Meyer's *Black Souls*. *Black Souls* ends with both white and colored bowed by the tragedy of race prejudice, but the heroic soul has been the black man's. It is a stirring, admirably conceived play, with the majority of the parts for Negroes, and doubtless will soon be known throughout the country. For the Little Theater movement has gripped the Negro's imagination, and it demands good Negro plays. One could write another chapter of the little theaters in Cleveland and Detroit, at Talladega and Fisk, and many other places.

I could not do it, for ill fortune has kept me from seeing any but our own Harlem Experimental Theater in New York. I am sure their work must be good, for New York has shown us all that the Negro actor is among the great entertainers of the world.

21 January 1933

Two of My Girls

$\mathcal{I}$ spoke in a previous chapter of two young men, Didwho Twe and Richard Brown, who had come into my life, who seemed especially interesting. I am speaking now of two young women out of the host whom I have known and for whom I have an affection. Such competent young colored women as I have seen grow up and take positions of importance! I like to remember that Richetta G. Randolph was my first stenographer, in the days when she lived at the Hotel Maceo and helped the weary minister, who needed aid with his bulky correspondence. Miss Randolph still takes an occasional letter for me, though she is now that most valuable person, the "undersecretary" as the English would say, to the secretary of the NAACP. But, if I should go over the long line of young people who have been so much to me in my chosen work, my readers would find it wearisome, and I would find, when I saw the list in print, that I had omitted some of the most important names of all! So, I am choosing only two, one whom I first knew in the past, one in the near present.

Carrie Lee, now Mrs. Blanchet, was brought up in New Bedford, Massachusetts, a pleasant New England town without visible sign of race prejudice. Negroes had always lived there and there had been no large influx from the South. At grammar school and high school, colored girls mingled naturally with white girls and were liked or disliked by their teachers without regard to race. So, when, in 1913, after passing entrance examinations for Smith College, Carrie Lee wrote to secure a room in one of the dormitories, she did not anticipate trouble. She had stated previously that she was a colored girl and the authorities would know for whom they were making arrangements.

But an unfortunate misunderstanding occurred. The president's office had the knowledge that Carrie Lee was colored, but the dean's office, where the dormitory matters were arranged, was not given this information, and the New Bedford girl of dark skin was assigned quarters with a girl from Tennessee.

When the Tennessee girl breezed into the room where Carrie and her mother were hanging curtains, a tragedy occurred. New Bedford, for the first time, came up against the unreconstructed South. The Tennessee girl went to the authorities and the authorities turned Carrie Lee out of her room. One of the professors, Miss Cavanaugh, took her in. So are good and bad mixed in this world! An insult brought Carrie Lee in close friendship with perhaps the best loved, finest spirit in the faculty.

A number of colored girls had graduated from Smith before this time, the most distinguished, Dr. Otelia Cromwell of Washington (Phi Beta Kappa from Smith, Ph.D. from Yale), but none had applied for dormitory privileges. Carrie Lee was the first girl to attempt to enjoy the full college life. Her people believed that life in the dormitory was an important part of the college training and sacrificed to give her all there was. But Smith was taken by surprise and for a time left the girl in an embarrassing position.

Her mother wanted her to pack up and come home. No college was worth the insult she had to bear, but the girl had the wisdom to wait. She did not give up and go to live, a considerable distance from her work, in the home of a colored family. That was what the authorities would have liked her to do. They did not want to have the issue forced upon them. She stayed and took such accommodations as the authorities would give, worked in one house for her meals, and stayed quietly near the college until, in the winter, she was assigned to one of the best dormitories on the campus. Her quiet persistence and her good standing in her work had put race prejudice to shame.

The NAACP had tried to help, but our protest did not win her cause. I heartily believe in protesting, but, on any matter that has a social side to it, it seems to strengthen the opposition. Carrie Lee got into the dormitory because of her character and of the friends she won. Neither aggression nor timidity would have won. It needed steady, unflinching persistence.

Throughout the four years of the college course many seemingly small battles had to be fought. All this, I want to say, was under President Burton, not President Nelson, the most liberal-minded college president today in the United States. There were conventions that meant little, and yet that must not be overlooked, lest it seem that the colored girl accepted an inferior place. I remember one: once during the year the seniors marched out from chapel two by two in the recessional. "Why couldn't Carrie Lee stay at home?" some of the girls muttered. "All the girls didn't appear." Carrie Lee marched out because she thought she ought to, and, when the situation was known, the president asked her to march with her.

I have said that I did not think the NAACP had anything to do with the decision of the dean's office that put Carrie Lee, at last, into a dormitory, but I think our support meant something to her through those four difficult years. For even during commencement week Nan Lewis, of North Carolina, had to sling an insult at the Negro in her Ivy oration. She was talking of the rural white South and then, with a little wave of her hand, said: "And as to the Negro, I refer you to the Negro minstrel show." I can feel now the little shock that went through the audience, and a girl near me whispered to her classmate, "Poor Carrie Lee." "She must have put that in at the last minute," another girl said as we went out. "That couldn't have passed the member of the faculty that read the oration." Nan Lewis was a conspicuous figure at commencement and evidently very popular. She has become a brilliant newspaperwoman and a radical and doubtless has learned to be ashamed of her early prejudice, but her influence at college must have been hard for a colored girl to overcome.

Carrie Lee wore the orchids that the NAACP board sent her on her graduation, and the letter that she wrote in thanks for all that we had done was so graceful and so sincere that one of the board said: "If college taught Miss Lee to write such English as that, I'll send my daughter to Smith." But something more than the English department made that letter what it was.

Well, here was a famous four years' battle that brought a girl, when it was over, near a nervous breakdown. "But what good came of it at last?" as Little Peterkin asked of the battle of Blenheim. Unlike Blenheim, the greatest good came. The decision was laid down in the dean's office that colored girls applying for dormitory privileges were to be given them. That matter was settled.

A number of dormitories since 1913 have received colored girls. White girls sometimes complain and learn that they may leave the dormitory if they wish; but, of course, as that isn't what they wish, they stay on. Harriet Pickens, a winner of athletic as well as of scholastic honors, lived at one of the newest and finest dormitories,

Gardner House. I was told that she was plastered over with orchids given her by enthusiastic classmates who had cheered their throats hoarse for her in the athletic events. She won this for herself, but she owed much to a former graduate who opened the door for her to enter.

I was in Seattle in 1928, speaking for the NAACP. I took cold as soon as I arrived and, with difficulty, kept my engagements; so, when Mrs. Hall, the secretary of the branch, asked me, on my last day, whether I would listen to a young pianist, I declined. The day was already full. I was to speak at three churches in the morning, was to dine with friends, to be followed by a reception in the afternoon, and to speak before a large audience in a white church in the evening. How could I do more?

Nevertheless, I went to hear the young musician. Lying on a couch in her pleasant room, I was prepared to hear an aspiring but mediocre player. That's what one generally hears at such a time, the world over. But after a few minutes I sat up. Lorenza Jordan Cole was no ordinary pianist. She had studied for three years under Mme Leiszniewska at the Cincinnati Conservatory of Music. Mme Leiszniewska was evidently a great teacher, and her pupil had been ready to work untiringly with hands and brain and spirit. The afternoon was glorified. To hear great music under the pleasant surroundings of a private home is a gift rarely bestowed upon the ordinary mortal.

I learned that Lorenza Cole had been recommended for a fellowship at the Julliard School in New York but had no private means, only a return ticket to Cincinnati. Impulsively, I told Mrs. Hall that, if she and her friends would raise money to help out for the first half of the year, I would raise it for the second half. Lorenza fell upon my neck, and I found myself assuming the responsibilities of a parent. It was the first time, and it looks as though it would be the last time, that I had had means to take up such grave responsibilities.

For, of course, a musical education could not end when a year was over. It took a second year to graduate. No one could have been more saving than my protégée, but it is not possible to live in New York without spending a considerable sum of money. But I was having a wonderful time. I was alone now, living in Greenwich Village, where I had a piano for Lorenza when she came to see me and where I heard the intricacies of Bach and the mellow loveliness of

Brahms, practiced over and over again. My neighbors on the floor below were considerate, and at the same time we were reasonable, and no complaint came from the practicing.

Lorenza Cole found the New York Institute of Musical Arts more friendly than Carrie Lee had found Smith College—but these were later days. I think, too, that among students studying an art there is more camaraderie than among college students, for art tends to obliterate both racial and national lines. Then the city is hospitable to anything new, and Harlem is a new experience to whites. Lorenza told me that she never went to a party that did not contain members of both races. Something of the charm that we hear so much about in Paris has come to stay in New York.

But race prejudices hit us both hard, and quite unexpectedly to me. The second summer, when Lorenza was preparing for a concert to be given in the autumn, the tenant below me sublet for the summer. I was leaving Greenwich Village to live uptown for two months and invited Lorenza Cole and her friend, Grace Postles, a graduate student at Columbia, to occupy the apartment, keeping a bedroom for myself when I should need it. I called on the newcomer in the apartment below, a young thing, lately married, and asked whether she minded practicing, and she said she should enjoy it. So, I went to the Springfield Conference of the NAACP feeling that everything would be all right.

In a couple of days I received a communication from my land-lord, asking me to request the colored women whom I had left in my apartment to leave. The people subletting below me were refus-ing to pay the original tenant, and he in turn was refusing to pay the landlord. I must throw the Negroes out.

Lorenza Cole told me that, when the landlord informed them of what he had done, Grace Postles, who wasn't disturbed whether the people below were insulting or not—she cared about her work and a place to do it in—asked Lorenza what she thought I would do. The answer was, "I don't know." "You see," Lorenza explained to me, "I had had instances like this and invariably the white person had gone with his race. He, or she, didn't want to, but the pull was too strong." I deserve no particular credit for standing by my convic-tions. I was giving up the apartment in October. I had the law on my side, and I was very angry. The landlord wrote some nasty letters, but, unless he could prove that the girls were a nuisance, he could do nothing, and he couldn't prove that. So, the young women stayed on. I visited them from time to time, and we gave a tea at the end, to which I, mischievously, invited the landlord's wife. It was a mistake, for it made the people below turn on their loudspeaker when our music began. But even that couldn't spoil our good time.

That same summer a complaint came in the apartment my sister-in-law rented against our having colored guests using the front elevator. It seemed as though New York, all at once, was going against me. But my sister-in-law managed the matter with decision and tact, and our guests were invited to use the front elevator again. When Mrs. Ovington had finished talking to the agent, he admitted that he had learned a good deal about the Negro and the different kinds of people belonging to the race. In a year we moved and made arrangements, before we signed the lease, as to how our guests were to be treated.

There is no settled policy regarding this elevator situation. It might be wise to bring up a case, but the case must be settled right, or infinite discomfort will ensue. Nearly everyone in New York lives in an apartment. The hallway and the elevator are really a part of the street. One's home is reached only at one's door. How to guard this inner street against annoyances without introducing caste lines is, I suppose, the problem. The line against servants, which I detest, is always drawn. In Greenwich Village I chose a house to live in with a single stairway partly to avoid the elevator situation, but I got into trouble just the same, and on a caste line. If I had said to a landlord that I had two maids taking care of my apartment, the Ku Klux gentleman below who used to yell up to the girls, "You niggers keep quiet," would have been satisfied. Probably, instead of squeezing against the wall, he would have joked with them as they passed him.

The concert came off, and, thanks to my many white and colored friends, enough money was raised for Lorenza Cole to study under Tobias Mathey for a year. She returned from London transformed. The New York Institute of Musical Arts has some great teachers, but it's run on the German military system. As one girl said to another as they stood outside the door waiting to be called in for an examination: "This isn't an examination in music, this is an examination in nervous endurance." Something was needed to supplement this, and my protégée returned from Mathey a different being, composed, secure, learned in the school that makes Myra Hess's playing carry us to the stars. For a week, Lorenza played for me at Dr. Alfred Myer's, who had most generously helped in her education, at Carrie Overton's in Harlem, at Edwine Behre's in Greenwich Village. I said good-bye with a sad heart. I wish I could get Los Angeles on the radio here in New York, for Lorenza Cole is living there and playing her lovely music to those great audiences that the air commands.

28 January 1933

The Pacific Coast

$\mathcal{W}$hen the Californian ceases to be a real estate promoter, the world will appreciate how beautiful his country is. But he still damns it with continuous praise. I remember one time standing in a garden at Taormina, looking at the huge rose bushes, not tidily kept like bushes in our parks at home, but wide spreading, careless in their loveliness. Suddenly I heard a high American voice: "I think it's foolish to cross the ocean and come to Italy to look at roses. Ours are so much finer in California. Why these ——." I moved away, anxious to put as great a distance as I could between us two. This was not the first time while in Sicily that I had heard such talk. Never, I vowed, would I visit a state full of blatant advertisers. But Branch work for the NAACP brought me to the Pacific coast and once there I felt the charm of climate and of people. The gardens that I visited, I may say, never equalled in beauty the old gardens of England or the Continent.

San Diego, the southern Californian tells you, has the finest climate in the world. We all have our tastes in climate, but probably few places have so equable, kindly climatic conditions, where one lives on regardless of the click of the calendar on a birthday morning. One of the NAACP's finest workers in that city, an elderly white man and a judge, told me that the city gently and tranquilly prolonged life. It was a few weeks after that that I had an experience at Long Beach, a sort of Coney Island for Los Angeles.

I went to Long Beach to speak for the newly formed branch. California towns often have community centers where halls of various sizes may be secured for meetings. At Long Beach there was a modest hall and an immense one that looked like a colosseum. This, the president of the branch declared, they had taken for me, and, when I expressed fear that the branch could not fill it (it could not have numbered more than a hundred members), I received a

113

grieved look and the explanation that the best only should be given the chairman of the board.

My worst fears were realized. It began to rain in the afternoon and by eight o'clock Long Beach was in the throes of one of those downpours that the Californian knows and doesn't advertise. The rain did not drop down; it fell down like water thrown out of a pail. And, as such rains occur infrequently, no proper sewerage provision had been made. It stayed in the streets, a noble torrent through which a few cars forded their way. Twelve people came to the great hall to hear me speak! After I had disembarked from the car and paddled to the door of the hall, I thought the gathering a large and courageous one.

I gave the people the speech I had prepared, much to their surprise, for I never could see why those who attended a meeting should suffer for those who stay away. At the end an elderly gentleman came up to me and said that, if I would return, he would promise to fill the hall for me. I looked at the enormous floor space and galleries and said that I would return. If he could perform such a miracle for an unknown speaker, I wanted to see it. He did perform it. When I came back a month later the hall was filled. And, still more wonderful, filled with men. Elderly men, who had lived long in the kindly climate at the Soldiers' Home for veterans of the Civil War!

Climatically, you can get pretty much anything you want in California—desert, snow-capped mountains, dry air, fog, if you prefer. The Pacific, with its dazzling sunsets, is more wonderful to civilized man than the Atlantic, since civilization ignores the sunrise. While at Carmel, in northern California, where I stopped to rest and write, I never ate between six and seven, preferring to pace the lonely beach, to watch the clouds, and to feel superior to the people who were dining behind closed doors. These people were friendly, however. All that I met, white and colored, were of moderate means, living, for the most part, in pretty bungalows, doing their own work, doing it together, and not bothering whether they got home in time for dinner or not. In such a paradise one should have found democracy, freedom from caste. One did, on the surface, but underneath one struck the rock of prejudice—against the Negro, the Asiatic, the workingman. Few states have been more cruel in their laws.

During my visit in 1921 I went to Imperial Valley to look into the Negro school situation. Of course, California has a compulsory education law, but at that time, when the Valley was developing its new cotton and dairy interests, colored children were not encouraged to go to school. Often the white teachers were quite willing to have them kept at home to work. Hundreds of Texans, white and colored, poured at this time into Imperial Valley, the whites believing in complete segregation, the Negroes reared in the school of taking what you can get. It was remarkable, though, how soon they began to make demands. We had branches at El Centro and Calexico working for better grammar and high school facilities. They were segregating the children and not encouraging them to go to high school. I went out to visit the ranch of one family from Texas and felt how much the new state had already done for its self-respect. Better wages made the battle for rights possible. I do not know how things may be in Imperial Valley at the present time; doubtless, they are suffering from the Depression like every other valley in the union, but I know the Negroes are not submitting to injustices without protest.

Interest in the association and what it stands for is common to the Pacific coast. In 1921 there was not a town with fifty adult Negroes that did not have a branch. Modesto was trying hard to get in, but it did not have that number of colored and could not persuade the white rancher to join. Wouldn't we let them in with 30 members, since they had a one hundred percent membership in the town? I moved down the great valley through which the railroad runs, visiting Stockton, Fresno, Bakersfield, instead of taking the tourist way by the coast. I was glad to see the fruit and vegetable farms. Cooperation made it possible for the small rancher to market the produce of his few acres as profitably as the large landowner. Everyone welcomed me where I spoke and showed their appreciation in taking out five- and ten-dollar subscriptions. We were just beginning, in 1921, to receive the larger memberships and the receipts were most gratifying. My only surprise was that more Negroes were not working the land.

In Fresno I met a farmer from Tennessee with forty acres of irrigated land. He employed a Hindoo. "I can't get a colored boy to stay," he explained, when I asked why he did not have as helper a member of his own race. "Negro boys don't like to emigrate. They lack the pioneer spirit; they get lonely and run back to smaller money and the old log cabin. They love home too much and mother." It seemed true that there were few young colored men farming. One reason might have been that, with the exception of some graduates of industrial schools, few had any idea of how this intensive cultivation, this careful, methodical irrigation, should be done. The many were too careless.

Delilah Beasley, author of the *Negro Trail Blazers of California*, would resent the statement that the Negro was not a pioneer. Her comprehensive study shows the colored man on the scene from the first Spanish settlement, through the days of Fremont and the Bear Flag, down to the present. Negroes were among the miners, they struggled for civil rights in slavery days, and they knew enough to buy land and hang on to it. Nevertheless, one sees very few, old or young, cultivating the land in California.

I reached Los Angeles at last and was welcomed by Mrs. Beatrice Thompson, then secretary of the branch. She took me to a colored home on a beautiful street, quite out of the Negro section, where I was taken care of by a dear old lady who came from Maine. She and her husband, who made violins in his leisure moments, passed for colored. This was my headquarters, and I moved from there up and down the coast, south to San Diego and La Jolla, north and west to Riverside and San Bernadino, to Long Beach and Pasadena, and more places than I can recall. The late R. Burton Ceruti was at that time the lawyer for the Los Angeles branch and a member of the national board. He was a very able man and a devoted believer in the Negro's full rights. Los Angeles has been fortunate in having a long line of able workers, and, when I returned in 1928 to our national conference, Dr. Claude Hudson was president of the branch, which outdid the East in the magnitude of its welcome. Never were we so comfortably cared for, for the Somerville Hotel was then completed and we lived in as charming a hostelry as one could find on the Pacific coast.

Northern California gave me as cordial a welcome as southern, and I lingered in the neighborhood of San Francisco for some time, speaking before student groups at the university, going to our various branches back and forth across the great bay, and making many friends. Flowers are gay and plentiful on the coast and my room was always filled with them. Mrs. DeHartt and the Bishops introduced me to many people. I met Anita Whitney, then under trial for membership in the Syndicalist party, and was delighted at the way the colored people were rallying to her defense. They might have little sympathy with syndicalism, but she was a friend and they meant to show their appreciation of her stand. There was a pleasant friendliness between colored and white in northern California that I missed in the South.

The Pacific coast has its branches north of California. I visited in Portland and Seattle and was introduced to the startlingly beautiful scenery by my many newly made friends. Certainly, the West does things on a royal scale.

And, if the scenery was regal, I found that some of the whites as well as the colored were generous in their attitude toward the race question. For it was in Portland that I first spoke before a gathering of Bahaists and learned that they were carrying out to the letter the commands of their prophet to obliterate race lines. I have since seen something of the group in New York, and I know their complete sincerity.

I suppose there are other national organizations in the United States so remarkable as the NAACP. I suppose so, but I don't really believe it! I don't believe there is another organization that has as many branches as ours, groups all over the land, functioning for those eternal rights of liberty and opportunity and equality that make men great. And functioning without pay. Sometimes a branch will be dormant for years, and then a man or woman will appear who has the vision and who calls it back into life. No wonder we have become a political power. When people will hang together, decade after decade, supporting an ideal, content only occasionally to come in contact with the few workers that the central office can afford, when they save from their small earnings to send a member to the national conference, when they respond to every appeal to action, then surely they are better than any other organization going!

I returned to New York via the Canadian Pacific, through those amazing mountains to St. Paul and Minneapolis, each with its cordial welcome, and then to New York. And New York looked dirty and dark. I had forgotten its many walls, its mere "tent of blue, that prisoners call the sky." I wanted the sun again.

4 February 1933

I Review Books

$\mathcal{I}$t was after extensive visiting NAACP branches and talking to many book clubs that I conceived the idea of reviewing books for our news service. Mr. James Weldon Johnson, our secretary, approved, and in 1921 I started "Book Chat." I wrote a review every fortnight until about three years ago, when I found that the colored papers were doing so much reviewing on their own account, spurred, I like to think, by my example, that I now only occasionally note a book. Moreover, the field has become so large that I cannot cover it.

In a previous chapter I spoke of the adverse writing that was dominant when I began my work. Magazines and publishers welcomed whatever Booker Washington wrote but rarely any other material. McClure, however, was an exception. In his magazine, beside the famous muckraking articles by Tarbell and Baker and Steffens, was poetry by Rosalie M. Jonas, best known now in New York by her verse, that each year brings in hundreds of dollars for a Christmas tree for colored children. In McClure's days she was writing "Piney Woods," a poem that was recited all over the country and is still the greatest indictment ever written against lynching.

Another verse that I remember was "The Jim Crow Car," [about] a Negro getting off the car rather than ride in it.

As Miss Jonas is white and comes from New Orleans, her work is of special interest. But she was before her time, as was also the best storyteller the Negro race has yet produced, the late Charles W. Chesnutt.

I had the chance to review a reprint of one of Chesnutt's books, *The Conjure Woman*. I wished it might have been "The Wife of His Youth," this short story from which the title is taken deserving to go down in classic American fiction. Chesnutt was not brought up in the South but went there as a teacher and told of what he saw. He wrote about colored people as white people write about white people, with little thought of propaganda. At least, he wrote like this at the beginning. His later novels were not successful because too much propaganda crept in.

Another novel written before "Book Chat" was James Weldon Johnson's *The Autobiography of an Ex-Colored Man*. I told Mr. Johnson, when I first met him, that he owed me ten cents in subway fares. Twice did I get on the wrong train at the express station, where I was standing engrossed in his story, and go to Bowling Green instead of Brooklyn. The third time, as I waited on the platform, I shut up the book! Like *The Conjure Woman*, *The Autobiography of an Ex-Colored Man* has been reprinted and is now in one of Knopf's series; so, years after the first reading I had the chance to review it. Of course, Paul Laurence Dunbar was long before "Book Chat," as was much of Du Bois's work. It's discouraging how the first writers are rarely surpassed.

In 1921 the white South was beginning to observe present-day conditions, and the first book I reviewed for "Book Chat" was Kerlin's *Voice of the Negro*. Kerlin was then a professor of English at the Military Institute in Lexington, Virginia. His volume was made up of quotations, chiefly from the press, giving the Negro's attitude toward his wrongs. (He did not remain long a teacher in Virginia.) It must have been startling to many white people. To the Negro it was everyday reading.

But the second book review was of different calibre. It also was by a Southern white man, T. B. Stribling. It did not voice opinion. It had little in the way of opinion; it showed facts, conditions in a Negro quarter of a town in Tennessee. It was called *Birthright*. Many of my colored friends did not like the book. Its hero was not heroic. But it showed conditions in the small Southern town with startling truthfulness. Before this the Southern stories fell into two groups, the "faithful servant and noble master" type and the "black brute" type. Men like Thomas Nelson Page and Joel Chandler Harris, who had known slavery in its mildest aspects and remembered it as children, wrote of Marse Chan and Uncle Remus and a kindly past. The North lapped this up. Later the black brute appeared in fiction, best known in Dixon's *Leopard's Spots*. This was also immensely popular.

But Stribling showed everyday conditions, took you into the quarter where the black people lived, showed the well into which the sewage of the town seeped and from which the Negroes must drink, above all, showed you the meanness of the white man.

In the old stories the white men were generous, but Stribling's white men openly cheated the Negro, from the cashier in the bank down. Mean, small, tricky—that was the white world that surrounded Peter Siner, when after four years at Harvard College he returned to his home. No wonder he failed and was lucky to escape with his life.

This was the beginning of realism in the Southern white's treatment of the Southern Negro. Clement Wood followed with *Nigger* and then came DuBose Heyward with *Porgy* and *Mamba's Daughters* and Julia Peterkin with *Green Thursday* and *Black April* and *Scarlet Sister Mary* and Carl Van Vechten with *Nigger Heaven* and, in South Africa, Sarah Millen with *God's Stepchildren*. How wonderful it was as the books came in numbers to my desk. Of course, some of the writers saw much more deeply than others, but all were searching with keen eyes and a desire to tell correctly what they saw.

And what were the colored writers doing?

The older ones were still writing polemics, but a younger group was looking about and soon joined the white novelists. First among them in importance was Walter White with his *Fire in the Flint*. Here, as with Stribling, the hero is a young Negro, fresh from college, who returns to his town to make a living. But Kenneth Harper, the young physician, is very different from Peter Siner, Stribling's indolent youth. Kenneth is full of confidence, anxious to begin work, believing that, if he minds his own business, he can get along in this Southern town. But, in the end, he is like Stribling's hero; this is just what he cannot do. Jim crow as much as you like, colored and white, rich and poor, the worker and the master, are bound to affect one another's lives. The tragic ending of Walter White's story leaves the field to the whites, but one knows it is only for the moment. The battle will be fought again and again until one side or the other is exterminated or until the two sides come together, resolved to live on an equality.

Fire in the Flint went through many editions. And each year novels come to me by Negroes, setting forth with some truth the life of the Negro world. I qualify the truthfulness because the educated Negro is afraid of his material. If he writes what he knows intimately, he has to look out of the corner of his eye at his people. "What will they think of me," he asks, "if I ridicule our group?" And out goes a bit of satire.

The race has been laughed at so much, abused so much, that it seems cruel to add to the dark picture; but, after all, colored folk are just as human as white, and the story that refuses to show them as they really are lacks virility.

I have a theory that the Negro has the misfortune to enter upon his literary career at the wrong period in the development of writing in this country. He is a pioneer. He is still slashing down the trees and building his log huts. He has faith and energy and laughter, and he is writing at a time when the dominant note is frustration. If, today, America adored Bret Harte and Dickens, then the Negro could go to the bottomlands of Alabama, to the hills of Virginia, to the riverboats of the Mississippi, to the slums of New York, and show the Fagins and Rogue Riderhoods, the Peggottys and Joe Gargerys, the Dick Swivellers and Sam Wellers, the little Nells and Mrs. Fezziwigs, a great galaxy of life, enthusiastic people, villains and hypocrites, heroes and clowns, loving wives and unfaithful ones, all of them drawn with romance and sentiment, sentimentality, if you will, but all of them with a zest for life. How we should laugh and weep, do everything but be bored.

But this is not the age of Dickens, and our Negro writers must use the form that suits their time. Some have achieved considerable success. The other day two different persons spoke to me of Jessie Fauset's novel *Chinaberry Tree*, men who have no interest whatever in the Negro but wanted to know whether I had read this appealing novel. You must realize that I am accustomed to speaking first of Negro books, and, when a white friend tells me emphatically that I must read one, I am more than pleased.

I did not find Nella Larsen's subtle stories as well received as I might have wished, but Rudolph Fisher's short stories in the *Atlantic* were greatly liked and his new detective tale is excellent. This is of interest because the plots of our Negro writers are apt to be thin, mere strings on which to hang a few incidents, like Claude McKay's *Banjo*.

But, if fiction has not yet brought the laurel wreath to the Negro writer, poetry has crowned him. I have reviewed three Negro anthologies in "Book Chat," Johnson's *Book of Negro Verse*, *Caroling Dusk*, and *The Brown Thrush*, an undergraduate work. But not only have the poets been gathered together; their separate volumes have achieved fame. Countee Cullen's *Color* rivaled Edna St. Vincent Millay's work in popularity. James Weldon Johnson's *God's Trombones* was a best-seller and still continues to have a steady demand. Langston Hughes's two volumes of verse, *The Weary Blues* and *Fine Clothes to the Jew*, brought him considerable notice.

Many volumes of verse come to my desk—Leslie Pinckney Hill, Georgia Douglass Johnson, Claude McKay, whose early work is his best; these and others I have read with deepest interest. And my acquaintance does not end with the reading. It has been no small part of my pleasure in my chosen life to meet the delightful group of Negro writers, young and old, who are contributing to the literature of the day.

Perhaps I dwell overmuch in these reminiscences on the importance of white and colored meeting on the high plane of endeavor, but to me it is the only way this question can be settled right.

Whether the contact comes through the workers meeting for a decent wage or the poets gathering to chant their songs to one another, prejudice disappears in a common interest. And, as the white writer reads his work that his admirers may hear his voice and know the sort of man he is, so the Negro writer cannot do too much of lecturing, of speaking at clubs and public forums. Countee Cullen has read to women's clubs all over the country and made personal friends and friends for the race. Langston Hughes, whose communism, we trust, will not dim his laughter, is a good comrade to all he meets.

Jessie Fauset continues to win that admiration that F.P.A. expressed years ago in his column when he met her after the publication of *There Is Confusion*. A good lecture bureau for Negro writers should help this idea along.

I have spoken of the polemic writing of the older generation, a type of writing that for the moment has gone out of fashion. But Kelly Miller's power of argumentation always strikes one as fresh and vigorous, and William Pickens's combination of humor and common sense delights his readers. Editorial writing improves all the time. The colored reporter is getting a mastery of his job. But this is away from "Book Chat," of which I started to speak. Of the reading of good books there should be no end, and of the printing of good books on and by the Negro, there seems to be a continuous supply.

I have left until the last the name of a man who had done more than any one person to bring the facts of Negro life before the American public: Carter Woodson.

Dr. Woodson, since the foundation of his *Journal of Negro History*, has, with a scholar's patience, endeavored to interest the world of educators in Negro history and to persuade the Negro public of the importance of correct documentation of facts regarding their race.

In this he has succeeded in a manner scarcely possible when one realizes his economic handicap. The Associated Publishers, as his firm is called, has sent me a number of books to review on history and biography and has published more that I have not seen. The books are full of important material and are making their way into the public school system. They should be accessible to all children, for our textbooks still leave the American child to the mercy of the Ku Kluxer and the apologist for slavery.

In Harlem we have at the 135th Street branch a Negro library, the gift of Arthur Schomberg. It is one of the great collections of the city, and there it is, open to the public, a place where he who desires may learn of the history and achievements of his race, may read the books the Negroes have written, and examine, if he be found worthy, the rare first editions. But how few go!

Its very accessibility probably makes it less appreciated. It is a collection made by a remarkable scholar whose generosity I can admire but cannot attain unto. To give from one's library one book that one loves, that tears the heart. Imagine giving away the whole.

11 February 1933

My Books

$\mathcal{I}$ have written just two things that have stirred people's hearts and for the moment brought me fame—a bit of free verse and a short story.

The free verse, "Mary Phagan Speaks," was printed in the early days of the *New Republic,* August 1915, and brought comment from all over the United States. One enthusiastic critic compared it favorably with Mrs. Browning's "Cry of the Children"! It was frequently copied (I was proudest that it headed F.P.A.'s column), and talked of for a month or so, and then forgotten as it deserved to be. It was fortunate enough to say the right thing at the right moment and to choose a simple, terse form of expression.

Leo Frank had been lynched for the alleged assault of Mary Phagan. My Mary Phagan spoke from her grave and asked the people of Georgia why they had not cared for her when she was alive, instead of spending so much money and murdering a man for her sake now that she was dead. Why had they put her in a factory instead of giving her an education? Why had they kept her so poor that she had not even a pretty dress? This question will always be a pertinent one, and, coming as it did at exactly the right time, it struck home. Naturally, it ceased to be remembered as soon as the incident of Leo Frank dropped from men's minds.

My second triumph was a story called "The White Brute," published in *The Masses,* November 1915.

The war in Europe stirred me more than I had ever been stirred before and made emotional work possible. I have kept Max Eastman's letter telling me how greatly he admired and wondered at my story. "It seems to me a classic and more terrible than anything but truth." Even now I may be introduced to some new person who gropes in his mind to find the connection with my name and then says: "Mary White Ovington? I remember, you kept me awake all night with a story of yours. I still cannot forget it." It was a stark tale, told me in a sentence by a white woman in Alabama, the raping of a colored girl, snatched from her husband as they waited at a railroad station. I gave it its setting and its end. The story was reprinted by the NAACP and thousands of copies were circulated. The late John Orth, musician, of Boston, was responsible for giving away hundreds of them. He used to distribute them to passengers on railroad trains when he was traveling! One gasps to think of a passenger on a train, going probably on some pleasant journey, having to read this terrible tale. But, then, he could throw it out of the window.

With these two pieces of writing my success ceases. Nothing else that I have done has stirred my audiences to anything but a pleasant ripple of interest or led any but the faithful to the buying of a book or the recommending it to library or club.

I would doubt my ability only that I have secured the best of publishers and have had reviews far beyond the books' deserts. But for this I should cover my typewriter, but I haven't a hundred pages of rejected manuscript. There must be something subtly wrong that doesn't show on the surface. I believe it is what I have spoken of in connection with colored writers, the deviation from the straight storyteller's course to look sideways at the colored audience and secure its approval.

I have five books to my credit and a little play, *Phillis Wheatley*, that I trust will become known and fill a want in church entertainment and school. *Half a Man* was my first publication, a study of the Negro in New York. It has made its way into many libraries. Its facts have never been questioned, and it is still used for required reading in some colleges. My second book is the only one that I paid for myself. The few publishers who saw *Hazel* felt that its interest would be chiefly with Negroes and they doubted the buying power of that public. I believed in the book, however, and, with the *Crisis* as publisher, printed this juvenile, the story of an educated little colored girl from Boston who went South to visit her grandmother. There were no bookplates and at the end of some years the two thousand copies were disposed of. I learned something by that business experience. I sent a hundred copies to a colored man of more enthusiasm than business integrity, who was confident he could sell them all. I never saw the books again or received any money and the colored lawyer whom I asked to look into the matter never made any report. If I seem to be somewhat hard on the Negro in business transactions, may I say that I read the *Afro-American* and know how the white man is accused of fleecing the Negro. Any of us can be fleeced, whatever our color, and I don't believe there is much to choose between the two races in chicanery or gullibility.

Hazel was liked by the children who read it, and now and then some young woman comes up to me after I have spoken at a meeting and says: "I read *Hazel* when I was a little girl, and loved it," and I feel far more proud than of any executive work that I have done. We're all foolish regarding our writing.

My next venture was a novel based upon a gorgeous theme, an illegitimate white child hidden among colored people. I knew one such case and I saw the dramatic possibilities. My white child was brought up by respectable, ambitious people who gave her an education and trained her in kindliness and good manners. A third of the way through the book she finds out that she is white and enters the white world. And there I made my mistake, bringing in the labor with the race problem and overloading the book, as writers of first novels are apt to do. *The Shadow* had a good start, and while it never sold heavily, it was read more than anything I have written, for it was serialized in an English magazine, an Irish weekly newspaper, and a colored newspaper. The English comments were especially flattering.

The Shadow was published in 1920. After that I devoted myself wholly to executive work for some years. But, when I saw nearly everyone at the NAACP publishing books and articles, the desire to be in the race again took hold of me. And again I looked sideways at my colored audience and asked myself what I could do that would help the cause.

Biography was in the air. Elizabeth Sargent had recently published a volume of short sketches of prominent people, among them Paul Robeson. Why not make a volume of short biographies, all of them colored? Mr. Johnson gave me my clever title, *Portraits in Color,* and I started on my task.

Nothing could have been more delightful than getting the material.

It took me to Chicago to see the editor of the *Chicago Defender;* to Little Rock to meet Scipio Jones; to Atlanta, where Marcus Garvey was serving a sentence; to Augusta and Lucy Laney's school; to Richmond and Maggie Walker, whose kindly appreciation has greatly heartened me; to Peak's Turnout, where Janie Porter Barrett is doing as worthwhile work as anyone in the United States; to

Tuskegee to see Dr. Moton and Professor Carver; while at Washington, I interviewed Dr. Johnson and Dr. Ernest Just. Everybody was kindness itself in giving me material and I took immense pleasure in my work.

It missed fire. My eyes were not straight ahead, intent on revealing character as well as achievement. "Success stories," Gwendolen Bennett called them, and with truth.

Biography today must have some spice to it if it is to succeed. I tried too hard to please. And yet, of those of whom I wrote, not half expressed any pleasure in the volume or took the trouble to acknowledge it, while one was openly indignant at not having been praised fulsomely enough.

A few friends, always loyal, pushed the book, but it evidently did not meet a need as I had expected. Everybody, colored as well as white, prefers the spicy or exciting story to the more homely tale of fine achievement.

My last book, *Zeke*, a juvenile, comes out during the Depression, when we are all questioning whether we can buy bread, not books. It's my best piece of writing. It is a story of Tuskegee and depicts a colored boy in his first year at school, his homesickness, his work, his disobedience to authority, his success at last. The reviewer in the *Saturday Review of Literature* ended his very flattering account of the story by saying:

> Mary White Ovington has brought to Tuskegee, thinly disguised as "Tolliver," additional fame. Known for years as the great Negro school founded by Booker Taliaferro Washington and renowned as an exponent of industrial training, Tuskegee will now have a niche in the Hall of Fame of boyhood fiction through "Zeke." The establishing of this kind of school tradition with its emphasis on honor and loyalty comes with the mature years of an institution and is an interesting development in the life of the school and the race.

Tuskegee felt quite the opposite, thought me disloyal in painting a boy who was naughty enough to play cards on a Sunday, and assured me that I was caricaturing the school. For while, to the outsider, the school has "mellowed and matured," the campus still wishes it viewed in terms of publicity leaflets, all its teachers perfect and all its boys hard-working, God-fearing students—a place of paragons.

Well, these are my books. I have had a happy time writing them, and they have brought me some recognition. I suppose I shall keep on writing as long as the urge continues, and I suppose also that I shall use Negro material. I try to write sketches of white people, but they won't come alive. But one resolve I have made. Hereafter, I shall look straight ahead at life. No side glances at the Negro world of opinion. A man must be described as a God if he shall be pleased with his picture, and a race must be pictured as constantly heroic if it is to be pleased with its portrait. Or is this only true of oppressed people? Probably. At any rate it's mighty poor art. The essay can be written showing only one side of the picture. But the creative work should reverently depict the reality in life. If it only shows success, it is less beautiful than if it shows weakness as well as strength. I did this in *Zeke*, and that is why it has been called vital, with "intimate knowledge of Negro school life and character." I hope to do it again.

18 February 1933

Conclusion

$\mathcal{I}$ reach the last installment of my reminiscences with a sigh, partly of sorrow and partly of relief at a task finished. When I started I meant to have the whole series completed by December, and here it is the middle of February, and I am pounding my much abused typewriter and trying to decide how to chose this desultory story. One must have a last word, but what shall it be?

If my audience were white, I should know that they would want me to answer the question, put with awe or severity, or just plain curiosity, "What is your solution of the race problem?" But I think my *Afro-American* audience has only a languid interest in such a question and its answer. They know, as we all do, that, with the "rapid transit" discoveries of recent days, the peoples of the world will ultimately become one. Some centuries from now we will be one race, and an ugly, mongrel race at that. But for the immediate future, in which one alone is really interested, one guess is as good as another. Changed economic conditions, a revolution, might for a time break down race barriers, but after the conflict is over the results are never what we expect. I always answer the question with, "I don't know."

I am apt, however, to be pressed for some generalizations; we all like to hear conclusions, and one or two occur to me now that may be of interest. My opinion is worth no more than that of any other observer who has studied the race question and lived close to it. It may be I am too close. But I do feel certain changes, especially changes among the whites.

It's about twenty years ago that I was introduced to a man of middle age, a Yale graduate, successful in law. We were at dinner together, not a big dinner with four hundred people all yelling at the tops of their voices, but a dinner where four people ate and conversed quietly at a restaurant. My work was mentioned, and the Yale man was genuinely interested. I spoke of the educated Negro, men-

129

tioning some with whom I had worked and noting Negro achievement. This was in a small city of the North, where there had been a recent political upheaval. My new acquaintance had helped to prosecute certain Negroes who kept disorderly houses. It was quite evident that he discounted everything I said. He knew that the black man was inferior. If, as I persisted in pointed out, the Negro had succeeded, as Booker Washington had succeeded, it was because of white blood. To him the American Negro, intellectually, was the African savage of whom he had read in his boyhood geography.

Should I meet him today, he would be bound to be different. I should not meet a wall of incredulity as I did before. Some information must have filtered into his brain through his business, through his philanthropy, through his reading, through his visits to the theater or to the concert hall. And also propaganda against Negro achievement has stopped, and he no longer reads of the inherent baseness and stupidity of the race. We need to remember that slavery could only be defended in the nineteenth century by making the slave akin to the brute. Propaganda like that was slow in dying, but, while it may still be in the background of many white men's minds, as definite teaching it has ceased.

Not that the whole truth is yet taught—the important place of the African in universal history is slow to be accepted. Professor Hansberry, of Howard, in one of his lectures, shows a volume of a popular history of Egypt where certain important Egyptian kings are pictured with Grecian features. The writer of the book could not bring himself to use pictures of Ethiopians when writing of the Ptolomies, so he substituted present-day drawings for the correct photographs taken from the tombs. Such foolishness will not last much longer. We have reason to believe that the recent discoveries of anthropologists and archeologists will make their way into our popular literature and we shall find the civilization of the Ethiopian taking its rightful place beside the great civilizations of Egypt and Assyria and Greece.

But, after all this has happened, as long as the Negro can be distinguished from the white by his physiognomy, we may have a race problem in America, and it may be a worse problem than that of today. A minority group doesn't cease to be persecuted when it becomes a rival of the white majority. Quite the opposite. One has only to look at the Oriental in California to understand that. If the Negro did not have so firm a foothold in the United States, he would have been thrown out long ago. But he can't be colonized and he can't be successfully segregated. There is absolutely nothing but his color—no past ingrained civilization, as with the Oriental; no religious difference, as with the Jew—to separate him from the white American. Can he be kept out of his rights for long?

Every now and then the members of the NAACP board begin discussing whether we should change our policy, whether there is a new note to be stressed. What it would be we don't know, but the youth of the race does not seem eager to support us. I, for one, stand where I did twenty-five years ago. If there is to be any distinctly Negro movement, it should still be on the lines of full citizenship. While we remain a political democracy, we must battle to get the Negro inside of the government, a voter, a member of a jury, an equal in every way before the law. If the revolutionists are correct and our government will change (if it does change, it is far more likely to turn Fascist than Communist), some other program may be necessary, but, while we are waiting, let us, as in the past, patiently bring cases of color discrimination to court, try to vote in the white primary, defend the unfortunate who is discriminated against because of his color. This is slow work, but perhaps, after continual, patient hammering, the walls will fall with a crash. That they have already fallen with a crash at a few individuals' hammering we know. They may suddenly tumble and a race may come in to the sound of trumpeting.

I began these reminiscences at my home in the country, and, despite today's winter wind and falling snow, my mind harks back to the country as I say good-bye. I used to expect to end my days in a tenement, living a life among working-class people, the trolley cars clanging under my window, the children's voices rising shrill, happy, above the city noise. One summer at the settlement I wrote a verse which I called "By the Playground," which the *Outlook* published. Jeering letters came from friends who disbelieved in my conclusion. But I was quite sincere. It went like this

> Which of the summer sounds
> Is sweetest to tired hearts?
> The low, unwearying hum
> Of the bee in the clover bed?
> The hymn of the thrush at dusk?
> Robins that call in the rain?

Cool waves slipping away
From the boat as she sails through the sea?
Whisper of wind in the wheat?
Or from the fresh-smelling field
Where the heavens are thick with their stars
The crickets' comforting chirp
Telling of welcome and home?

Hot winds carry the sound
Of the city's traffic and cries,
While from the little square
Come the voices of children in song,
Hundreds of children at play
Circling and singing their glee.
Glad in the gift of today,
In the sunshine and warmth of the earth.
In the joy of youth but begun,
Chorus of mirth and goodwill,
Childhood's treble of hope.
This is the summer sound
The sweetest the tired heart knows.

It may still be a sweet sound, but, with the blossoming of my apple trees, I turn from the possibility of hearing it to the country. The need, for my peace of spirit, to leave New York's walls, its reverberating noises and hurricanes sweeping down its narrow canyons, has come with the years. I have taken Voltaire's advice and turned to cultivate my garden.

My "garden" is four acres in the Berkshires. On it stands a three-room cottage, made over from a barn. It boasts a pump for its plumbing, and in the spring grass has been known to grow between the cracks of the concrete floor. It looks like nothing from the front, facing the road, but the rear, with its little low windows and door, might be the cottage Hansel and Gretel came upon where the wicked witch lived. I hasten to say that I have no oven into which I might entice a visiting Hansel, only an oil stove on which to cook the midday meal. Out of its door one steps at once upon the grass to see a lawn and apple orchard and below the bank a meadow edged by the Green River, of which Bryant wrote. Some might call it a brook, but it has a noble swimming hole.

As to the literal garden, the place of vegetables and flowers, I spent too many summers "by the playground" ever to learn successfully how to cultivate the soil. Still I HAVE raised peas and beets, lettuce and beans. Whether they would have equalled my neighbors, I was not allowed to know. With an unfaltering belief in my altruism, the woodchucks and the rabbits took everything. Rabbits not only love the peas of commerce; the sweet pea is also their delight. Indeed, there are few flowers which they do not appreciate in the bud. So, of recent years, I think of my garden in terms of wildflowers and meadow grass, elm trees and lilac bushes, apple orchard and locust hedge.

Some of my enjoyment I owe to my friends. A year ago, on my retiring from the chairmanship of the board, our NAACP branches presented me with a gift of money to use as I pleased. I put it into my garden, into those extra things I would never have did not some lovely surprise shower down upon me. I wish more of my friends would come and enjoy them, my lounging chairs under the trees, my afternoon tea table, my comforts within doors.

Everyone who takes the Mohawk trail passes through Great Barrington, my nearest town. Call me up from there and come in at five o'clock and have a cup of tea, or come earlier for a swim in the pool.

The old interests still hold me. When this is printed I shall be starting on a field trip for the NAACP in Ohio and Indiana, ending in Nashville, Tennessee. As always, I shall feel the thrill of meeting loyal workers, of experiencing whole-hearted, thoughtful hospitality. I came across a letter the other day among some that my mother had kept. It was written to her from California in March 1921. In it I said: "Yesterday I was saying to myself a poem I used to love to recite at about seventeen:

> I wait for my story, the birds cannot sing it.
> No, not one, as he sits on the tree.
> The bells cannot ring it, but long years, oh, bring it
> Such as I wish it to be!"

Certainly, my wildest dreams would not have given me such a wonderful life as I now have.

So, I close these rambling chapters with an appreciation of the work that I chose, written at a time of happy voyaging in the cause of human brotherhood. Robert Louis Stevenson gave as his Desiderata: "Health, one or two hundred a year, and Ach, Du lieber Gott, friends." I have had all these, and among the friends none have been more precious than those of another race than mine. That the sincerity of my friendship has never been doubted has been my greatest joy.

25 February 1933

Mary Phagan Speaks

In 1913 Leo Frank, a Jewish factory supervisor in Atlanta, Georgia, was charged with the death of a thirteen-year-old pencil factory worker, Mary Phagan. When he was convicted and sentenced to death, appeals to higher courts failed. Citing evidence unavailable to the jury, the governor of Georgia commuted Frank's death sentence to life in prison. On 16 August 1915, a group of men from Marietta, Georgia, Phagan's hometown, seized Frank from a state prison, drove him to Marietta, and lynched him. Two weeks later the New Republic published "Mary Phagan Speaks." Rebuking the maudlin sentimentality that led to the lynching, Ovington's Mary Phagan speaks from her grave to the "men of Georgia," who were passionately aroused by her death but cared so little for her in life. When a witness to Mary Phagan's death offered testimony to his innocence in 1986, Georgia's Board of Pardons and Paroles exonerated Leo Frank.[1]

You care a lot about me, you men of Georgia, now that I am dead.
You have spent thousands of dollars trying to learn who mutilated my
    body.
You have filled the columns of your newspapers with the story of my
    wrong.
You have broken into a prison and murdered a man that I might be
    avenged.
But why did you not care for me when I was alive?
I was a child, but you shut me out of the daylight.
You held me within four walls watching a machine that crashed
    through the air,
Endlessly watching a knife as it cut a piece of wood.
Noise fills the place—noise, dust and the smell of oil.
I wish some of the thousands of dollars that you spent on the trial
    might have kept me in school,
A real school, the kind you build for the rich.
I worked through the hot August days

When you were bossing the girls, or shooting birds,
Or lounging in doorways cursing the nigger;
And you never paid me enough to buy a pretty dress.
You sometimes spoke coarsely to me when I went to and from my
    work;
Yes, you did, and I had to pretend I liked it.
Why did you despise me living and yet love me so now?
I think I know. It is like what the preacher told me about Christ:
People hated Him when He was alive,
But when He was dead they killed man after man for His sake.

Note

1. "Mary Phagan Speaks," *New Republic* 4 (28 August 1915), 101; republished in *Current Opinion* 59 (October 1915); 269–70 and elsewhere. See also Leonard Dinnerstein, *The Leo Frank Case* (Athens: University of Georgia Press, 1987); Robert Seitz Frey and Nancy Thompson-Frey, *The Silent and the Damned: The Murder of Mary Phagan and the Lynching of Leo Frank* (Lanham, Md.: University Press of America, 1987); and Nancy MacLean, "The Leo Frank Case Reconsidered: Gender and Sexual Politics in the Making of Reactionary Populism," *Journal of American History* 78 (December 1991), 917–48.

The White Brute

Following the Atlanta race riot of September 1906, Mary White Ovington toured Georgia and Alabama, comparing racial conditions there with those she was studying in New York. After visiting Atlanta, she traveled through the countryside, where she studied peonage and visited rural Alabama settlements managed by William Benson at Kowaliga, Charlotte Thorn at Calhoun, and Booker T. Washington at Tuskegee. Ovington also met a few white Alabama dissidents, including Joseph Manning, a Republican newspaper editor at Alexander City, who had been beaten for publishing articles sympathetic to black people. One evening in a darkened parlor Mrs. Manning described "an unforgettable incident of white brutality," which, Ovington said, "burned into my consciousness." After an extraordinary encounter with the Socialist Party's state secretary in Birmingham, Ovington left by train for New York.

As her train moved through north Alabama's barren landscape, Mary White Ovington was depressed by recollections of Mrs. Manning's story about the rape by white men of a black woman, whose husband could only stand by helplessly. "We ran past a forlorn little station with WHITE and COLORED over its two doors," she recalled many years later. "It might have happened here," Ovington thought. When she returned to New York, Ovington wrote "The White Brute." It appeared in Max Eastman's periodical, The Masses, eight years later, when the NAACP was battling the image of the "Black Brute," promoted in D. W. Griffith's enormously popular motion picture, The Birth of a Nation. The impact of Ovington's short story hinges on a reversal of the image of the "black brute," as the usual excuse for lynching.[1]

It was a very hot day, and the Jim Crow car was the hottest spot in the State of Mississippi. At least so Sam and Melinda thought as they got out at the railroad station to change cars to go to their home.

"Come out of the sun into the shade, Linda," he said, when, a heavy bag in each hand, they started to move down the platform.

"I ain't minding the heat," she answered, smiling up at him.

He looked down at her, his dark eyes gleaming from his black face. He was a large, powerfully built man, with big muscles under his newly pressed coat and strong hands that showed years of heavy work in the fields. He swung the two bags into one hand and with the free one drew the girl to his side.

"You's the sweetest thing," he whispered.

Again she smiled up at him and her eyes were very soft and dark. Her new straw hat, with its blue ribbon, rested for a second on his shoulder. Then with a little laugh she started down the platform.

"We'll come inside," she said.

They entered the small, ill-ventilated room marked COLORED. It was a dingy place, for the stove in the center still held the winter's ashes, and the floors were thick with many weeks' dust. At one end was a window where the ticket seller would come a little before train-time to serve, first, the whites from their window in the adjoining room and, last, the blacks from theirs. But no one was about now, and the two settled themselves upon the dusty bench. The girl, with a little yawn, leaned back against the wall.

"Reckon you is feel sleepy, honey," the man said tenderly. "You was up all night mos'. We sure had the finest weddin' in the country. Your folks ain't spare nothin'. I never see so many good things to eat nur so many pretty dresses befo' in all my bawn life."

His bride slipped her hand in his. "We wanted to give you a good time."

"You sure did. It was the grandes' time I ever knowed. Dancin' and ice cream and the people a-laughin' and the preacher a-hollerin' with the res'. And all the while my li'l gal by me and me knowin' she was mine furever an' ever, ter have an' ter hol'."

He pressed the hand that she had given him. "I can't see why you took me, Linda. Tom Jenkins is a preacher and learned in books, and I ain't nothin' but a black han' from de cotton fields."

She pulled his necktie into place, and then, glancing at the door and seeing that there was no one in sight, she drew his black face close to hers and kissed him.

"Tom wasn't much," she answered. "You're so big and strong. You make me feel safe."

He gazed at her and still wondered that she had chosen him. He knew himself to be uncouth, uneducated, scarcely able to read the sign over the doorway, while she had been to school for two years, had worked for white folks and knew their dainty ways. She had

lived in a town with many streets and could not only read the newspaper, but could sing hymns out of a book. Then she was slender,
with a soft brown skin, wavy hair, and small hands and feet. When
she smiled and spoke to him, he felt as he did when the mockingbird
told him that winter was gone and he caught the first scent of the jas-
mine bloom. How could he ever show her his great love?

He longed to perform some service and, noticing a tank in
the corner of the room, walked over to get her some water. But, as
he turned the spigot, nothing flowed into the dirty glass. The tank
was empty.

"That's mighty mean," he objected. "Looks like they ain't
know a sweet little gal lak you was comin' hyar. Jos' wait a minit an'
I'll git you a drink."

Leaving her for a few seconds, he returned, an anxious look on
his face.

"De train am late," he declared.

"Of course it's late," she answered a little petulantly. "I've lived
near a station all my life and I never knew a train to be on time.
Sometimes it's an hour late, sometimes twenty-four."

"Dis ain't so bad as all that. Dis train am two hours late. De
ticket man tole me so."

"That means nearly three hours here. Well, cheer up, Sam.
We'll get home sometime, and then you can show me our house
with the roses growing over the po'ch—"

"And de clock—"

"And the worktable that you made—"

"And de turkeys—"

"And the cooking stove—"

"Yes, ma'am, don't you forget de new cook stove!"

She laughed and rose to her feet. "Let's go outside," she suggested, "perhaps there's a breeze there."

They left the dirty room and walked upon the platform. Up the
track was their freight depot, where were piled bales of last year's
cotton crop, not yet moved. A Negro lay on a truck fast asleep.
Across the track was a group of tumble-down shanties, the begin-
nings of the straggling little town, with its unpainted houses and
fences in ill repair. Only the church, raising its slender spire back of
the houses, gave an impressive touch to the village. To the right the
platform belonged to the whites, and two men lounged against the
wall. They were young fellows with coarse, somewhat bloated faces

that betokened too much eating of fried pork and too much drinking of crude whiskey. Both were chewing tobacco and expectorating freely upon the floor. One of the men carried a gun.

"Suppose we cross the track," Melinda suggested, "and see if we can't get some sarsaparilla. It would taste good."

"I reckon I wouldn't go 'bout hyar much, Linda. Dis ain't no place fur you and me. De whites is mighty mean and de bes' of the cullud folks is lef' town after de lynchin' hyar twenty years ago."

"A lynching, Sam?"

"Yes, they got him outen one o' dem houses right over yonder and tied him to a pos' down de road a bit. He warn't a *bad* feller, but he done sassed de sheriff—wouldn't let him 'rest him widout a fight—and dey is burn' him alive."

"No, no," the girl cried, and turned a frightened face toward her husband. "Sam, it won't be like that where you live?"

"Don't you be 'fraid, honey. De white folks is fine down my way if you treats 'em right. I know; I worked for 'em for years 'til I bought my lan'. Now I pays my taxes reg'lar, and when I comes along, dey says, 'Howdy, Sam,' jes' as pleasant lak. I neber put on no airs, jes' alys pertend as deir cotton am a heap better'n mine, dough it ain't near so heaby, an' we gets along fine. I can't never fergit dat lynchin' dough," he went on reminiscently. "Pop brung me to see it, hel' me high in his arms. It warn't much of a sight fur a little boy though, de roarin' flames an' de man screaming—how he is scream—and the flesh smelling lak a burn' hog."

"Stop!" the girl cried. "Don't tell me anymore, it's too horrible."

"I won't, honey. In co'se it ain't for a li'l gal lak you to hear. So you sees I ain't lak dis hyar town much. But we'll go on over dat-a-way and take a walk. It can't do no harm."

"We won't go far, Sam, and you must talk about something pleasant. About the cooking stove, eh? You haven't once told me about the new cooking stove, have you?"

"Don't you be makin' game of me!"

"Get the bags, dear. We don't want to leave them lying about."

"In course we don'. Somebody mought open 'em an' steal dat white weddin'-dress. But 'twouldn' be much widout you in it. You was shinin' lak a li'l white cloud lyin' close down to de black yearth dat's me."

"Oh, go along," and she gave him a shove.

He was gone a few moments and when he returned he saw that

the two white men had walked over to where she stood. She hurried swiftly toward him and he noticed that she was breathing fast.

"That's a right pretty nigger," the taller of the two men said to Sam. "Belongs to you, does she?"

"Yes, sir," Sam answered. "She's my wife. Jes' married las' night," he added in a burst of confidence and pride.

"Don't look like it," the white man answered. "She ain't black enough for you, nigger. What are you doing courting a white girl like that?"

Sam threw back his head and laughed. "You sho' is funny," he said.

"Let us go, Sam," Melinda whispered, tugging at his arm. Her face showed both anger and fear and she tried to walk with him across the tracks.

But the men stood directly in her way. The first one went on: "Don't you all be in a hurry. You don't live here, I know that. Reckon we know every nigger in town, don't we, Jim?"

He turned to his friend, who nodded assent.

"Enjoying your trip?" He addressed the bridegroom, but his eyes traveled, as they had traveled before, to Melinda's slender figure and soft, oval face.

"Yas, sah, we's enjoyin' it all right. We's waitin' fur de train now ter take us home."

"What train?"

"De train from the South, sah. Ought to be hyar by two o'clock, but it ain't comin' til fo'. Pretty po' train, to keep a bride waitin'." He showed his white teeth again in a broad smile, but his eyes were fixed anxiously on the white man's face.

"That's a right smart time to wait, ain't it, Jim?" The man with the gun nodded. "Reckon we ought to do something for your amusement. Give your girl a good time now?"

Sam laughed again to show his delight at the man's facetiousness. "You's mighty good, sir, to think about my girl and me. But we don't need no amusement. We ain't been married long enough to be tired of one another, has we, honey?" and he looked down into Melinda's face.

She was terrified, he could see that clearly. Pulling at his arm, she drew him back toward the waiting room. "Come in here, I want to sit down," she said.

Sam led her into the room only to find the white men following him. Standing at her husband's side, the girl turned and for the first time spoke to the men.

"This room is for colored," she said.

The man with the gun spat upon the floor, but did not move. The other, with an ugly look coming into his thin, unhealthy face, answered,

"There's plenty of places where a nigger can't go, my girl, but there ain't a place where a nigger can keep a white man out, least-aways in this county of Mississippi, ain't that so, Jim?"

"That's so," was the other's answer.

"So, listen to what I'm saying. Your train leaves at four?" turning to Sam.

"Yes, sah," was the answer.

"Don't you worry, then. I'll bring the girl to you all right. Won't let you miss connection. We wouldn't part husband and wife, but I mean to have my time before you go."

Sam felt the girl's hands about his arm in a grip of terror. Her hot breath was upon his cheek. Patting her two hands with his big ones, he whispered, "Don't you worry, honey."

Then he looked at the men and laughed a harsh, scared laugh. "I knows white folks," he explained, speaking to her and to them. "I knows dey don't want to do us no harm. They jes likes to play wid us, dat's all. Niggers kin always understan' a joke, can't dey, boss?"

"This ain't a joke," the white man retorted sharply. "We-all mean what we say. We ain't jawing at you all this time for nothing. Give us the girl right quick or we'll hang you to the nearest pole and shoot at you till you're thicker'n holes than a rotten tree full of woodpeckers."

"A nigger ain't much account here," the man with the gun added, shifting his weapon in his hand. "We shoot 'em when we feel like it. There's a law for shooting coons. We burned a nigger here twenty years ago. Got a souvenir of him. Want to see it?" And he thrust a hand into his pocket.

"Sam!" the girl cried.

He looked into the face that had smiled upon him a few minutes before to see her sweet mouth drawn with fear and her eyes starting with terror. His fists clenched and his body stiffened, ready for the battle. He measured the man with the gun. He would strike him first, and then, the weapon secured, he could easily shoot his companion. Or he would squeeze those lean necks, one in each hand, and see the eyes start out from the bloated, ugly faces. He would kill them before her, his mate, who had chosen him as her protector.

And, after that, what?

As he stood there, alert, tense, ready to strike, before his eyes there flashed the picture of a man tied to a post, writhing amid flames, while to his nostrils came the smell of burning flesh.

His hands unclenched. Pushing his wife behind him with a dramatic gesture, he threw out his arms and appealed to the two men.

"I know de white folks is master hyar," he cried. "I ain't never said a word agin it. I's worked for the white boss, I's ploughed and sowed and picked for him. I's been a good nigger. Now I asks you, masters, to play fair. I asks you to leave me alone wid what's mine. Don't touch my wife!"

For answer the man with the gun struck him down, while the other seized the woman. Reeling against the wall, he saw them drag her to the platform, and when he had stumbled from the room he watched them disappear among the shanties across the tracks.

"Got your girl, eh?" a jeering voice said.

The question came from the Negro who had been asleep upon the truck, and who now sauntered over to where Sam stood. The outraged husband fell upon him in a blind fury, and beat him with his big fists until the other cried for mercy.

"Get out, then," Sam bellowed, flinging the bleeding man from him. "Get out, if you don't want me to kill you."

The man muttered a curse and slunk away.

"I'm sorry for you," a voice said at Sam's elbow.

The Negro turned again with raised fist, but dropped his arm and stood in sullen silence as he saw a white man at his side. The newcomer had emerged from the waiting room and was looking at Sam in friendly sympathy. He was an elderly man with white hair and beard and kindly blue eyes.

"I'm right sorry," he went on. "I saw 'em just now and it was a dirty trick. I'd like to have done something for you, but, Lord, you can't stop those boys. They own the town. Everyone's afraid of them. Jim there, he's shot and killed two, white men I mean, not counting colored, and Jeff's his equal. They ought to swing for it, but Jeff, he's the sheriff's son.

"You done just right," the man continued. "If you'd a struck either of 'em you'd be a dead man by now—or worse. They won't stand for nothing from a nigger, those boys. I's right sorry," he said over again, and, seeing that he could be of no service, he went on his way.

The black man in his strength and his helplessness waited on the platform through the interminable hours. The trainmen looked at him curiously as they went about their work, and, occasionally, a colored passenger spoke to him, but he seemed unconscious of their scrutiny or their words. His frenzy had left him and he stood, keeping silent watch of the shanties in front of the church spire. Once, when a train stopped and shut the town from his view, his eyes dropped and he stooped and picked up the bags at his feet, but there was no bright presence at his side, and, as the cars moved out, he put the bags down again and resumed his patient watchfulness. And, while his eyes rested upon the dingy outline of the unkempt town, his vision through all the hot, gasping minutes was of a dark-faced, slender girl in the clutches of a white brute.

The men kept their word. As the train from the South drew up, they hurried her onto the platform and pushed her and her husband into the Jim Crow car. "Good-bye," they called and then, with lagging steps, walked to the village street.

It was late afternoon when the bride and bridegroom reached their home. The western clouds were turning from flowing gold to crimson and all sweet odors were rising from the earth. Violets grew in the grass and honeysuckle clambered over the cabin side. At the porch was a rosebush covered with innumerable pink blossoms. And, as though he had waited there to greet them, a red bird chirped a welcome from the windowsill.

A moment's glow of happiness shone in the man's face and he turned to his wife. Vaguely he felt that the warm earth and the gentle, sweet-scented breeze might heal the misery that grieved their hearts. They had been like two dumb, beaten creatures on the train, bowed and helpless. But now they had quitted the world of harsh sounds and brutal faces and were at home. The man drew a deep breath and stood erect as he opened the door for her, but the woman crossed the threshold with shrinking step and bent head.

It was such a homelike place. All winter he had worked for her, fashioning a table for her use, placing a chair here and a stool there, saving the brightest pictures from the papers to pin against the wall. The dresser was filled with blue and white china bought with money he had taken from his own needs. Many a time he had gone hungry that they might have something beautiful on which to serve their first meal together.

"Sit down, Lindy, lamb," he said. His deep, rich voice had never been so tender. "Rest yo' hat and coat. I'll git the supper tonight."

He set about his task, lighting the lamp, kindling the fire in the new stove, and cooking the evening meal. But she ate nothing. She would startle violently at the fall of a log in the stove, at the leaf tapping on the windowpane, at the cry of a bird.

"That ain't nothin' but the tu'keys, honey," once he said soothingly, as he saw her tremble, "they's goin' to roost. They'll be right glad to see you tomorrer."

Presently, she arose and, in a hoarse voice, told him that she would go to bed. He led her into the little chamber that he had built for their bedroom. Setting the lamp that he had carried on the table, he looked up at her, his eyes asking wistfully for a caress as a dog might look at its master. But she turned away and he went out to keep his watch alone.

Sitting in the room which he loved and had fashioned for her sake, the clock ticking upon the shelf told him with every second of the happiness that he had lost. "Looks like I's 'bleeged ter bear it," he whispered to himself, "but it ain't right. It ain't right. No man had oughter treat anudder man lak dat. Seem lak dey think a black skin ain't cover a human heart. O God, it ain't right!"

When he crept into the bed beside her, he found her shaking with sobs.

"Honey," he whispered, "I's glad you kin cry. Let the tears come. Dey'll help you ter forget."

He would have laid her head upon his breast, but she drew away.

"Lindy," he cried passionately, "I was nigh crazy to help you, don't you know dat? I could hav' kill dem wid my two han's. But it wouldn't have been no use! It wouldn't have been no use! Can't you see dat? If you jes' thinks, you'll understan'. I'd seen dem burn a nigger as had struck a white man. Dat's what dey'd have done to me. Can't you see? You wouldn't have wanted to have seen me lak dat?

"And what good would it have done? It wouldn't have made no difference. You'd have had to suffer jes' de same. Listen, honey, I couldn't help you; it'd been jes' de same, only you'd have been lef' all alone.

"But you ain't alone now, Melindy, honey lamb, you's got me, and I'll toil for you from morn till night. I'll tend you if you're sick lak's if you was my baby chil'. There ain't nothin' I kin do fur you as I'll leave undid. Oh, Melindy, I'm here *alive;* don't you want me? I'm alive. You wouldn't rather have a dead man than a live one, would you?"

He stopped panting and listened for her answer.

At length it came in whispered gasps. "I don't know, Sam; I'm afraid. Every minute I'm afraid."

"Don't be afraid," he cried impetuously, throwing his arm about her. "I'm hyar."

And then he stopped. She had not turned to him but snuggled close to the wall, as if seeking protection there.

Outside were the soft night sounds, the vines rustling against the window, the insects' drowsy chirps. Far off by some distant cabin came the howl of a dog.

"A dead man or a live cur," he said to himself, and turned upon his face with a sob.

Note

1. "The White Brute," *The Masses* 6 (October–November 1915): 17–18; republished in Mary White Ovington, *The Walls Came Tumbling Down* (New York: Harcourt, Brace and Company, 1947), 88–99. See also Everett Carter, "Cultural History Written with Lightning: The Significance of *The Birth of a Nation,*" *American Quarterly* 12 (Fall 1960): 347–57; Joel Williamson, *The Crucible of Race: Black-White Relations in the American South since Emancipation* (New York: Oxford University Press, 1984), 140–79, and *passim.*; Ralph E. Luker, *The Social Gospel in Black and White: American Racial Reform, 1885–1912* (Chapel Hill and London: University of North Carolina Press, 1991), 135, 165–66, 183–90, 289–93, 295–301; and Ovington, *The Walls Came Tumbing Down,* 80–87.

Afterword

$\mathcal{I}$n this last decade of the twentieth century, the entertaining and insightful reminiscences of an almost forgotten woman, Mary White Ovington, have at last been rescued from the microfilm of aging newspaper copy and made available to contemporary readers. Ovington's years—from the end of the Civil War to five years after World War II—were fraught with change in everything from the bulk and length of women's dresses to weapons of mass destruction. Yet, more than sixty years after she wrote these reminiscences, her concerns remain astoundingly current. We are still questioning whether integration or separation is the best strategy for "equality" across the color line. We are still debating feminism, pacifism, and antiracist movements. We are still arguing about the power of art in all its forms to persuade and about questions of propaganda and censorship. And these are not the only issues Mary White Ovington confronted directly and with growing wisdom through her life and writing.

Reading Ovington's reminiscences, we may be stirred to ask other kinds of questions: What makes an individual devote a life, for no material reward and at high personal risk, to a cause and a community, outside her own? Is there a useful strategy one can learn for balancing ideals and practical goals? What can one learn from someone who has lived such a balanced life and has reflected upon it? What were the sources of strength and sustenance inspiring this work year after year, decade after decade?

These informal, serially published reminiscences were written when Mary White Ovington was sixty-seven years old. Her life's value, as she saw it, came with maturity, long after the fleeting days of teenage dating and dancing. She was thirty-two before she decided definitely not to marry and found satisfying work in settlement houses. Seven years later, she began what would become her life's work, moving from a settlement house in the immigrant

147

community of Greenpoint, Brooklyn, to conduct research in one of Manhattan's black communities in 1904. When she lived in the Tuskegee Model Tenement, the only white person in the neighborhood, she was forty-three. She was forty-four when the NAACP was founded; she became chair of its board at age fifty-four and treasurer at age sixty-seven. At eighty, she attended her last board of directors meeting in March 1946. Her name was first absent from its list of officers in 1948, when she was eighty-two.

When Carl Murphy, editor of the *Baltimore Afro-American*, convinced her in 1932 to write for his black readership, she was undoubtedly influenced by her need for money. Her account books indicate that she received two hundred dollars, paid in four installments from September 1932 to March 1933, for writing these reminiscences. The increasing impact of the Great Depression and the death of her older brother, Charles, in 1930 had slashed the Ovington Gift Shops family income which had sustained her modestly through her life until then. Once she was convinced someone was interested enough to pay her to reflect on her life, she enjoyed doing so.

The audience for the original publication of these reminiscences in the Baltimore paper was the leadership of the black middle class across the United States. Ovington knew her readers well from her extensive travels to NAACP branches, and the time was right for reflections about the NAACP's interracial history. By the time Ovington left as chair of the board at the end of 1931, she might have seen a larger justification for the extravagance of writing about herself. Against increasing despair about integration, about the ability, sincerity, or efficacy of white allies in the struggle for black civil rights, she would erect a vantage point of personal politics intertwined with historical change.

Thus in 1932 Ovington aimed to explain her departures from the norm for women of her race, class, and age. She wanted to emphasize that those departures did not result in a life of pain and suffering, but one of fulfillment, joy of work, and sustenance of community. Ovington agreed with Jane Addams that "nothing so deadens the sympathies and shrivels the power of enjoyment" as ignoring and restraining youth's impulse for "doing good." Correspondingly, when a person finds an outlet for "helpfulness" against "the starvation struggle which makes up the life of at least half the [human] race," one's own life is made happier, not more difficult.[1] Ovington did not want her audience to forswear any potential allies in work for justice. And for those who might follow her steps across false societal barriers, she intended to convey her experiences honestly, in positive terms that would encourage others to do likewise.[2]

The Walls Came Tumbling Down

Though Ovington was not young in 1932, her activity then does not suggest the physical struggles with aging which would hit her with a vengeance during work on what has until now been the most accessible of her autobiographical writing: her 1947 book, *The Walls Came Tumbling Down.* Between 1944 and 1947, she struggled with strokes, loss of eyesight, a deep (and uncharacteristic) depression, institutionalization, shock treatments, total loss of memory for half a year, a fall, and a broken wrist, and yet still managed to finish that work, her last great gift to the NAACP and the black community.[3]

The Walls Came Tumbling Down is more the story of the NAACP than it is Ovington's own story. She wrote it under constraints of health and audience which make it far different from the earlier reminiscences, less personally revealing, less optimistic, less open. While describing periods during her tenure as chair of the board and treasurer, for example, she foregrounds the executive secretaries: three of her eight chapters are focused on John Shillady, James Weldon Johnson, and Walter White.

Her emphasis on the organization she founded came from her perceptions of duty and audience, as well as her own modesty and ideas about what was important. The only pay Ovington received for her forty years with the NAACP began while she was hospitalized before finishing *The Walls Came Tumbling Down*, when the board voted to give her a two hundred dollar per month stipend. Contrary to the way she is often portrayed in histories—as comfortable, even upper class, with no money worries—she was desperately in need of funds by this time, and she was determined to "serve the NAACP" by writing its history. She did not expect the 1947 book to appeal to a white audience—they would want "the Negro's own story." She thought it would be of most interest to the unheralded black women in the NAACP branches across the country, as she put it, "Mrs. Jones of Muskegee, Mrs. Smith of Keokuk." This audience, she believed, had "rarely been reached, but it should be reached," and these women who knew her would like the "style of writing, semi-biographical."[4]

Though *Walls* is a thorough account of the Association, it does not answer our questions about Ovington's own sources of inspiration and energy. To find Mary White Ovington the person before and beyond the NAACP, we must look to these delightful weekly installments of her "reminiscences," the word itself suggesting wide-ranging, organically organized memories. We also must read between and beyond the lines, pulling out "the Truth" that Emily Dickinson says must be told "slant" lest we all go blind.

Reminiscences of a Life

In Ovington we have someone who took supposed limitations of difference, of marginalization, and turned them into tools for good, not for her own advantage, but for those she chose to serve. In writing, as in speaking, she was effectively subtle, gentle, and tough. She loved challenging work, and she thought little of self-promotion. Over and over again, she responded to kudos with wonderment that she should be praised for doing what she most wanted to do.

Time and again, in these chapters, Ovington reveals the settings of her accomplishments, but is silent about what she does, and does very effectively. A prime example is her fund-raising. She tells us she belonged to several organizations that led to the founding of the Urban League in 1910. She tells us she helped found and manage Lincoln Settlement in Brooklyn. She tells us that she was chair of the board of directors of the NAACP while Johnson was executive secretary. What she doesn't tell us is that she was fund-raiser for those early, formative organizations; that she raised the money for the Lincoln Settlement for over ten years so that the Head Resident could focus on programming; that she was instrumental in raising fifty thousand dollars for the Arkansas peonage cases alone while she chaired the board; that throughout the 1920s and 1930s she traveled across the country raising funds for the NAACP, never taking expense money if she had not raised considerably more than her travel costs.

Jill Ker Conway has pointed out that in autobiographies of several prominent women in the Progressive Era—Jane Addams,

Charlotte Perkins Gilman, Ida Tarbell—self-representation is flatter in their narratives than in their diaries and letters, with the latter reflecting ambitions, struggles, and managerial accomplishment absent in the autobiographies.[5] Ovington's narrative shares this reticence.

Ovington sought, found, and built upon the best in both individuals and organizations, and to this personal precept we may credit her ability to pull into common networks very different and sometimes very egotistical people. When Oswald Garrison Villard, Joel Spingarn, and Du Bois quarreled during the early, struggling years of the NAACP, Ovington kept them working together so that the organization could survive. "Few can encourage ability without dominating it," she says about Jane Addams (6). She might have included herself in the select number.

Ovington was able to succeed in the new and venturesome enterprise of "Settlement Work"—more than she, of course, indicates herself—because of her healthy curiosity and her ability to enter and ultimately identify with people imaginatively whatever their differences, a state of mind which never left her. Her seven years as head of the rapidly expanding Greenpoint Settlement in the huge Astral Model Tenement (which still stands in a neighborhood now entirely Polish), lent her enormous insight into the lives of working-class women ("mother-managers," she called them admiringly), and girls (whose temptations toward prostitution were entirely understandable to someone intimately in touch with the reality of their only alternative work—Greenpoint's jute mills). Ovington emphasizes her move toward socialism at this time, her introduction to "the worker's party" by the men of Greenpoint and the intellectuals of the Social Reform Club. But her later castigation of the Socialist Party for its failure to support women's rights, as well as her refusal to let the Woman's Party deny black women's rights in order to gain the vote for white women, had its roots, very likely, in her visionary understanding of working women in Greenpoint, and her recognition that these harried, hard-working women had no one to speak up for them.

"I Begin My Investigation," Ovington titles the chapter about her move into the black world after her second social shock: that the conditions for New York's black populace were worse, even, than for its white immigrants. Here, and in the following chapters, "Two Leaders" and "Living on San Juan Hill," what she fails to tell us is what a formidable researcher she was. She gives no inkling that she led, not followed, Mary Simkhovitch and the Greenwich House Committee of Columbia University professors into studying, and then instituting programs for, black Manhattanites. Ovington's elegant, breakthrough sociological study of 1911, *Half a Man: The Status of the Negro in New York*, thrice reprinted,[6] gives us solid information about children, women, health, work, morality, and living conditions from 1904 to 1911, as well as holistic research methodologies for understanding—and strategies for improving conditions within—communities. Her shorter work published at the time was groundbreaking, too. When *Charities* editor Paul Kellogg asked Du Bois for his opinion of an Ovington submission, "The Negro Home in New York," to the social service journal, thinking the article too positive, Du Bois wrote back, "I have no criticism to make of this excellent article."[7]

In her relationship with and influence on Du Bois, Ovington's modesty, her concentration on cause, not self, must be acknowledged. She tells us of their early correspondence, and admits that, looking back at the file of letters (which Du Bois's most recent biographer, David Levering Lewis, calls the great leader's most chatty and revealing), she was rather free with criticism. The two very quickly moved from the roles of worshiping admirer and condescending leader to collegial interaction. It was Ovington who nudged Du Bois away from some of his "Talented Tenth" dependence to a serious flirtation with socialism in the years after 1910, long before his better known adoption of communism late in his life.

Ovington gives us wonderful pictures of the 1906 meetings of Du Bois's Niagara Movement at Harper's Ferry and Booker T. Washington's Negro Business League meetings in Atlanta, both of which she covered as a reporter for the *New York Evening Post*. The image of Richard Greener doing a double take in the South after seeing this same attractive, blond, blue-eyed forty-year-old in the audience for his very contrasting remarks in the two places is priceless.[8]

The image Ovington conveys of herself in these descriptions of the "Two Leaders," Washington and Du Bois, is of an interested observer, privileged to be watching history in the making. The larger truth is more complicated and could reveal her influence in the significant shift from Washington's low pressure, accommodationist stance to Du Bois's demands for full equality. Since Washington increasingly controlled black newspaper outlets, her reports of the

Niagara Movement meetings of 1906 and 1907 provided their most favorable coverage in U.S. general readership publications; her reports of Washington's Negro Business League subtly undercut his leadership and dominance. As Ovington wrote to Du Bois, she had reported "with all fairness," but had praised Washington only *"through other people's mouths"* (Ovington's emphasis). She had tried to get her reports published elsewhere, too, she told Du Bois, but "I made it too clear as to just where the point of division between the two Negro camps lies." Washington wanted "to keep this fuddled, and what Dr. Washington wants still goes—'But not for long, oh, not for long,'" she added.[9]

Ovington briefly mentions muckraking journalist Ray Stannard Baker and his *American Magazine* articles that became his 1908 book, *Following the Color Line.* She does not mention the campaign she waged to move Baker into a more liberal position on questions of race relations, in person and by mail, in an attempt to inspire favorable coverage of Du Bois in the popular media. Nor do Baker's biographers take any note of the many letters from Ovington in his papers, letters recommending people to see, places to go, questions to ask, care to take in order not to endanger informants.[10]

Thus Ovington is left out or only briefly noticed in much of the history written about the important decade leading up to the founding of the NAACP in 1909. In fact, she deliberately turned her invisibility as woman and as not wealthy (as compared with *Post* editor Villard and Ovington's friend, industrialist and journalist John Milholland) to her advantage. Because she was not a target of Washington's sycophancy, nor yet an object of his spy networks and disinformation campaigns, she was able to write, publish, speak, influence, and keep pushing money and media and fence-sitters like Villard and Baker toward Du Bois's side. Perhaps her recognition of the effectiveness her lack of prominence lent her is part of the reason that Ovington did not, in 1932 and 1933, fully explain her own role in events leading up to the NAACP founding, nor her central role in the survival and success of the organization during its first twenty years. In an unpublished foreword written by Walter White, then secretary of the NAACP, for Ovington's 1947 book, he describes the effect of her subdued but strong style:

> Her delicately pale blue eyes, her placid and sensitive face, and her beautifully tailored pastel clothes leave breathless and defenseless

those who meet her for the first time after becoming angered because of her views. When, instead of the grubbily dressed, fanatic-eyed, loose-moralled female which neurotic enemies always picture in their minds as typical of those who speak out for minorities, such visitors to Miss Ovington's office find her quite different, it is usually some time before they can gather their wits together enough to launch the planned attack. When her cool and incisive wit and wisdom [are] brought into the discussion, Miss Ovington's erstwhile foes are changed into friends.[11]

In her 1947 book, Ovington pairs the Cosmopolitan Club Dinner of 1908, one of the events that led to the founding of the NAACP, with a dinner at the Inter-Collegiate Socialist Society. There she heard Lucien Sanial, who had "stood with the workers during the Paris Commune." "Well-fed, well-dressed," she reports, she and her socialist friends stood and sang William Morris's "March of the Workers" (to the tune of "John Brown's Body"). Sanial looked at them and said (in Ovington's words): "Remember, you can be of no use to the workers, [not of the] least use, unless you repudiate your class, absolutely repudiate it; and even then . . . even then, most of you would be useless."[12]

Ovington describes going home "profoundly disturbed." She believed "that the economic problem is civilization's first problem, and that the workers' rebellion against their lot is the most profound fact of history." But she knew, too, that "I was only cheering and throwing a few pennies." Thus she resolved that "I would cease to work for socialism and give what strength and ability I had to the problem of securing for the Negro American those rights and privileges into which every white American was born. Thus the Negro, *if he willed it*, should be able to march with the working class" (emphasis added).[13]

Why is this "resolution" which, she says in 1947, "seemed important to me at the time," left out of the reminiscences? By 1932 Ovington was repeatedly disappointed that most blacks who had attained some measure of economic security showed little interest in marching with the working class. In 1918, both privately and publicly, she expressed her disillusionment. "Sometimes I wish I had had the courage really to join the labor movement, to forsake father and mother and sister and brother and live the life of the working class," she wrote to Joel Spingarn. "These folk who play with unionism or socialism until it hits their little world and then drop it returning to the viewpoint of their class, are of little use. At any rate I knew enough to know that and so went in for the Negro, where I could use what I had. But it troubles me sometimes lest we are only helping to make a black bourgeoisie."[14]

And she complimented A. Philip Randolph and Chandler Owen on their magazine, *The Messenger*, which "makes as its cornerstone the solidarity of labor, and the absolute need of the Negro's recognizing this solidarity." As a longtime socialist, she told them, she had looked in vain for Negro college graduates "imbued with the revolutionary spirit"; happily, here in New York were two good college-trained socialists "who are giving up their life to the spread of socialist thought." "Class consciousness, internationalism, these alone can save the black races of the world," Ovington believed, and, indeed, World War I had "shown that they alone can save all mankind."[15]

The operative phrase in her resolution of 1908, remembered in the 1940s, was "if he willed it." Even as pressures for the NAACP to turn to economic issues began to mount from the left in 1932 (in her concluding chapter Ovington mentions only board discussions of "whether we should change our policy"), she recognized that the NAACP drew its support from the black middle class across the country; it could not drastically change its program from civil rights legal activism to economic agitation and keep that support base. Ovington's audience in 1932 was not particularly interested in her early resolve to make it possible for them to join the workers' movement. And so she left such matters out of her reminiscences.

In her reminiscences, Ovington's narration of the founding of the NAACP differs somewhat from the story she told in an oft-reprinted pamphlet, *How the NAACP Began*, written in 1914, when the organization was still walking the tightrope of neither allying itself with nor allowing a fatal enmity toward Washington and his many powerful followers. It differs, too, from the formal history she published in the *Journal of Negro History* in 1924. "It's legitimate now to raise the curtain a little," she can write in these reminiscences (56), long after the death of Washington in 1915. But we see only the skeleton of the Washington–Du Bois conflict: we do not see the narrator's encompassing work in the founding of this gutsy, unique organization in 1909.

Ovington drew together a group of people known for their

power and positions, whether because of their money (Milholland, Sears Roebuck head Julius Rosenwald, Joel and Arthur Spingarn, Villard); or their radical identity (Milholland again, Charles Edward Russell, William English Walling); or their passion for justice and social welfare (Addams, Ida Wells Barnett, Du Bois, Moorfield Storey, Lillian Wald); or their educational and academic reputations (Franz Boas, John Dewey, Livingston Farrand, John Hope, E.R.A. Seligman, Vladimir Simkhovitch, Burt Wilder). She does not mention that she was the singular individual who was capable of capturing their interest and commitment, who could hold them together, and who could keep the organization alive. But the fifty-three signers of "The Call,"[16] issued on Abraham Lincoln's one-hundredth birthday, 12 February 1909, were friends, colleagues, or acquaintances of Ovington—from the Unitarian Church, from Harvard, from settlement work and social work, from the Social Reform Club, from her Greenwich House research committee of Columbia University professors, from her contacts in the black community (and beyond) over the previous five years, from journalism, and from the Socialist Party and the Inter-Collegiate Socialist Society. While many of them did not know each other, they knew her.

Having pulled these people together to meet, to educate themselves (an emphasis of the conference which can also be credited to Ovington), and to form a permanent organization, Ovington continued to work behind the scenes. She kept them working together. She knew how to look for and foster the best in each human being. She minimized her own importance and raised the visibility of Villard and Du Bois, Walling and Russell. In "The West Indies," she notes that upon her return from her obligatory family trip to Jamaica in 1910, she found written in meeting minutes "that the entire matter of the coming conference go over until Miss Ovington's return." Elsewhere she wrote that at first she was provoked by this, but then realized that "I was the only one among the white and colored board of the Association who had plenty of leisure and at the same time a conviction that this was the most important work that she could do. So, dropping all interest not Negro, I gave time—the one thing Moorfield Storey or Oswald Villard or Hutchins Bishop did not have—to the Association's needs."[17]

Perhaps "Studio Days," more than any other single piece of Ovington's writing, reveals the integration in her own life which enabled her to work single-mindedly for the NAACP, even as she did other kinds of things. As she describes her work beyond the NAACP, it is always linked to it: her completion of *Half a Man;* her work on the excellent anthology for high school readers, *The Upward Path,* published by Harcourt Brace in 1920; her support of the young painter Richard Brown; her administration of Lincoln Settlement. But, as she says, "My studio was a place for play as well as work," with international visitors, dinners, dancing. "We were not always discussing the race problem," she remembers (71), but readers conversant with the Mabel Dodge–type arts salons of the teens will recognize a level of inclusion in Ovington's gatherings not evident in the more self-indulgent rebellions of others. In Ovington's studio, race, class, nationality, gender, and occupational divisions were ignored. And "fun," which Ovington repeatedly emphasized as necessary to life and work (remember her wanting to put the young parson in Winston County, Alabama, into "citizens' clothes," to send him to a "nice dance"? [46]) was well-blended into the mix of people. Her studio days continued through many decades of her life, as they continue in her reminiscences even after she left her spacious Brooklyn studio, in her fascination with the stage ("The Stage"), in her adoption of the young pianist Lorenza Cole ("Two of My Girls"), in her book reviewing and writing ("I Review Books" and "My Books").

In Ovington's chapters devoted to her travels—to the South ("I Go South," "The Far South," and "Northern Alabama"); to the West Indies; to London and the Races' Congress; to the Pacific Coast, and especially California—we also note her integration of work, play, learning, and writing. For, as she briefly indicates here, she invariably used her travels, even when obligatory for her family or concentrated on NAACP activities, to do more than relax or work only for the organization. Perceptive publications flowed from her travels to Puerto Rico and Algeria with her mother in the teens.[18] Stories and articles she wrote about her travels across the United States throughout the 1920s include such unique reportage as an extensive, on-the-scene description of the midwife training program in Mississippi funded by the Sheppard-Towner Act.[19] Reading, traveling, thinking, and writing all contributed to Ovington's leadership and wisdom, and especially to the NAACP's development, as it became increasingly bureaucratized and isolated in New York City in the 1920s.

More must be said of Ovington's books than she tells us in "My Books." *Hazel* (1913) and *Zeke, A Schoolboy at Tolliver* (1931) were written for a young black audience long before diversity was a watchword and while negative caricatures of blacks dominated both young adult and adult fiction. The books illustrate her skill (they are very good reading) and her awareness of such issues as the use of dialect, which she rejected in an attempt to reproduce vernacular speech. Taken together with her edited reader, *The Upward Path*, these works foreshadow the extensive, knowledgeable, and forward-looking study she made of public school textbooks in the late 1930s as head of the NAACP's Textbook Committee.

Ovington dismisses her 1920 adult novel, *The Shadow*, much too readily, describing as "a mistake" her incorporation of labor issues into the very clever reversal she makes of "passing" literature, with her white protagonist raised as a black child. In fact, the plot allowed Ovington to give an overview of many differing attitudes toward race in the South and the North and gave her the opportunity to suggest narratively what she had concluded in her own life's work: that for the black American, race discrimination must be ended before one could make common cause with the workers of the world.

In her 1927 collection of biographies, *Portraits in Color*, are exceptional sketches of some people whose names we recognize; of some accomplished but nearly forgotten women; and of many whose names we should know, but probably don't. Ovington came close to winning a Pulitzer Prize for this book. One suspects that the reason she did not has much less to do with its quality than with its subject matter; as with all of her work, it was far ahead of its time. Until the end of her life, Ovington received letters, many from schoolchildren, thanking her for these "portraits in color."

Writing a Woman's Life

Lives as well as works have themes. The clear theme of Mary White Ovington's life is the struggle for integration in all its senses. She is a force in U.S. history, in her NAACP work and in her personal life, as she fought to remove legal and social barriers to black people: integration in the racial sense. On a personal level, she integrated a happy, healthy childhood and youth with an active recognition of pain and suffering in the world. And in her genuine joy in difference, in difficulty, and in hard work, she was able to bring together disparate people and principles to work for practical, principled ends: integration of yet another kind.

The supportive theme to this amazing life is longevity— longevity in years, in ideals, in work, in engagement across the stubborn barriers of race, class, age, gender, and nationality. In her reminiscences we get an insider's story of formative questions and periods in U.S. history. Less directly, we sense the long-standing, undergirding life structures that enabled Ovington to keep going while atrocities such as lynching repeatedly shattered her public world, and strictures of an aging body narrowed her private capabilities.

In writing of her life, Ovington gives us stories of the external world, the world of doing more than of thinking or feeling, and mostly the public external world—at her time, a male world. But one of the first things one notices in her life is that she acted always as a female, sharing and revealing, indirectly when not directly, those characteristics of group identity imposed by her culture and differences in socialization resulting from gender. Susan Stanford Friedman has pointed out the general difference in male- and female-authored autobiographical texts as being individualistic versus interdependent within community.[20]

Ovington was not concerned with defining or integrating a "self" in this writing.[21] That was something she found particularly self-indulgent. She criticized the kind of individualistic, intimate, sexual revelations omnipresent in Emma Goldman's two-volume *Living My Life* (1931), published near the same time, as well as undue emphasis on one's inner life. Popular autobiographical writing of the time, Ovington thought, centered too much on "thought life," "perhaps . . . because civilized life has to be so circumscribed." A record of thoughts alone was not worth much, she believed.[22]

The thoughts or the writings of Mary White Ovington were only important, in her thinking, as they took shape in actions in the world. In "fleshing out" what she thought could be of interest and importance, Ovington was bound to present external result rather than internal motivation. This characteristic she shares with Addams, who prefaced *Twenty Years at Hull-House* by stating her primary goal: "Because Settlements have multiplied so easily in the United States I hoped that a simple statement of an earlier effort . . . might be of value in their interpretation and possibly clear them of a certain charge of superficiality."[23]

Certainly Addams's work is the first which comes to mind in

relation to Ovington's reminiscences because of the emphasis of both women on their chosen causes rather than on themselves. But there are clear differences between their memoirs. In a recent collection of women's autobiographical writing, Jill Ker Conway includes Addams in a section titled "Pioneers and Reformers" and notes the romantic cast that ambitious and accomplished women place on their life stories, suggesting always agency outside of themselves.[24] Ovington's narrative noticeably lacks this romantic outside agency, probably as a result of her strong Unitarian training in the primacy of reason over emotion.

We have noted with Friedman the "collective identity" of women as a "source of strength and transformation."[25] This is where we come to a key difference between Ovington's life story and those of the women with whom she is compared: the elderly, Progressives, radicals, the privileged. Ovington indeed identified with and defined herself by community, but she reached across the lines of race, caste, class, gender, age, and historical period to identify differently both in imagination and with committed action. Her difference from Addams was one of degree; beginning in the 1890s, Addams, Ovington, and others such as Simkhovitch and Wald stepped into the world of immigrants and the poor.[26] In 1904, Ovington alone among women of her time took a step further into territory forbidden and enforced by U.S. custom and law.

Marginalization comes in many shapes and forms, in many ways and times of life. Marginalization of a woman's life story may come when men write histories; marginalization of black history may come when whites tell the story. Ironically, the correctives of black studies and women's studies have until now left out Mary White Ovington, a founder of the premiere U.S. civil rights organization. As a white woman, she escapes black histories. Not a woman who put white women's rights first, she is squeezed to the side of those histories. Saddest of all, as a believer in the validity and joy of the altruistic life, her story has been erased by sometimes cynical assumptions that the only legitimate or effective spokespersons on oppression are victims.

As we struggle through today's cacophony of causes and cancers that recycle through U.S. history, let us be grateful for the still, small voice of these reminiscences. "I suppose the miracle is always here if someone will come to call it forth" it says (52). Critical examination of autobiography has moved from evaluation of the quality of the life and the veracity of the writer to centering on questions of self-representation—defining the genre, categorizing the types—and more recently to emphasis on narrative artifice and reader response.[27] With reader response the critical vogue of the day, the conclusion of Ovington's story lies with us. Arlyn Diamond, in writing of women of the civil rights movement of the 1960s, quotes one of them, Elinor Langer, as saying that "American radicals have never been able to reach each other across the decades very well."[28] May this republication of Mary White Ovington's quietly told but astounding story extend our historical and personal reach.

Carolyn E. Wedin

Notes

1. Jane Addams, "The Subjective Necessity for Social Settlements" (1892 paper), *Twenty Years at Hull-House* (1910; reprint, New York: New American Library, 1961, 1981), 90–100.

2. The *Baltimore Afro-American* republished Ovington's 1932–33 Reminiscences after her death in 1951. By that time, the needs of the audience that Ovington clearly had in mind when she wrote the pieces had intensified, leading Murphy to preface each installment with a box headed "Why We Print This Story." Readers were told that Ovington was "no fair weather friend," and that "the race problem was no fad with her." "She shared the problems of the race from days when it was almost a crime for white people to associate with colored people."

3. Kathleen Woodward, in her study "Simone de Beauvoir: *Aging and Its Discontents*" (in Shari Benstock, ed., *The Private Self: Theory and Practice of Women's Autobiographical Writings* [Chapel Hill and London: University of North Carolina Press, 1988], 90–113), reminds us that aging has not received necessary critical attention in autobiographical studies. Looking at the constraints Ovington knew writing *The Walls Came Tumbling Down* reveals much about the ways in which focusing outside of oneself might make pain manageable as well as production of art still possible.

4. Mary White Ovington (henceforth MWO) to Arthur Spingarn, 16 October 1946, NAACP Papers, Library of Congress. Ovington even worried about, and received some criticism for, using the first person in *The Walls Came Tumbling Down*. See Walter White to MWO, 31 July 1946, NAACP Papers, Library of Congress.

5. Jill Ker Conway, "Convention versus Self-Revelation: Five Types of Autobiography by Women of the Progressive Era" (paper presented at the Project on Women and Social Change Conference, Smith College, Northampton, Mass., 13 June 1983), as referred to in Carolyn Heilbrun, "Non-Autobiographies of 'Privileged' Women: England and America," *Life/Lines: Theorizing Women's Autobiography*, Bella Brodzki and Celeste Schenck, eds. (Ithaca and London: Cornell University Press, 1988), 62–76. Heilbrun concludes from Conway's points that there is "no model for the female who is recounting a political narrative" (70).

6. Reprints of the 1911 publication include Schocken Books's "Sourcebooks in Negro History," with a new preface by then NAACP head Roy Wilkins, and by Negro Universities Press, both in 1969; and by Hill and Wang in 1970, with an introduction by Charles Flint Kellogg. The foreword to the original publication was written by anthropologist Franz Boas.

7. MWO to Louise Ovington (her mother), n.d. ("about 1906" has been written on the letter in what looks like MWO's script; more likely the date of the letter is fall 1905), box 8, folder 4, MWO Papers, Archives of Labor and Urban Affairs, Wayne State University. The published article appeared in *Charities* 15 (7 October 1905): 25–30, in a special issue, "The Negro in the Cities"; Du Bois also published an article in the issue.

8. Greener, whose consular appointments and other jobs had been obtained through Booker T. Washington, was the latter's primary spy at Harper's Ferry.

9. MWO to W.E.B. Du Bois, 10 September and 20 September 1906, Du Bois Papers, University of Massachusetts.

10. See Robert C. Bannister, *Ray Stannard Baker: The Mind and Thought of a Progressive* (New Haven: Yale University Press, 1966; reprint, 1979), and John E. Semonche, *Ray Stannard Baker: A Quest for Democracy in Modern America, 1870–1918* (Chapel Hill: University of North Carolina Press, 1969).

11. Walter White, "Introduction to *The Walls Came Tumbling Down*," box 10, folder 28, MWO Papers, Wayne State University. Ovington edited out all the physical and detailed description of herself in White's foreword; thus the published version calls her "Fighting Saint," briefly mentions her "modest disclaimers," and says she "marched serenely ahead" to save white America's soul, black America's body.

12. MWO, *The Walls Came Tumbling Down* (New York: Harcourt, Brace and Company, Inc., 1947), 47–48.

13. Ibid.

14. MWO to Joel E. Spingarn, 5 April 1918, Spingarn Papers, New York Public Library.

15. MWO, "Letter to *The Messenger,*" *The Messenger* (July 1918): 114–15.

16. Fifty-three people are listed as signers of "The Call" in Ovington's version; sixty names are included in the version in Villard's papers.

17. MWO, unpublished typescript, box 1, folder 27, MWO Papers, Wayne State University.

18. MWO, "Algiers: In the Land Where the Sons of the Desert are the Children of France," box 3, folder 34, MWO Papers, Wayne State University; MWO, "The United States and Porto [sic] Rico," *New Republic* (8 July 1916): 244–46; (15 July 1916): 271–73.

19. MWO, "Catching a Baby" [1928–29], eleven-page typescript, MWO Papers, box 6, folder 35, Wayne State University. There are many letters here recording Ovington's attempt to have this article published in *Good Housekeeping,* where she thought it would do the most good in saving the Sheppard-Towner Act. Mississippi had engaged in a remarkable plan of empowerment with its federal aid. Most of the state's population, black and white, was brought into the world by 4,209 midwives, 99 percent of them black, most elderly, illiterate, and incompetent. Recognizing their importance to their communities, the State Board of Health gave these women licenses to practice under state supervision and trained them. Ovington narrates her visit to a rural log cabin meeting of the "Mississippi Mid-Wives Association" which concluded with an inspection of the midwives' bags and the singing of eight verses of "The Midwives' Song," to the tune of "John Brown's Body."

20. Susan Stanford Friedman, "Women's Autobiographical Selves: Theory and Practice," in *The Private Self,* 34–62.

21. See Marjanne E. Goozc, "The Definitions of Self and Form in Feminist Autobiography Theory," *Women's Studies* 21 (1992): 411–31, for a very helpful overview of "ten important books on women's autobiographical writing" published since 1980 which address the "overriding and recurrent concerns: the interrelated issues of self and form." Early analysis of women's autobiographical materials emphasized discontinuous forms and fragmented selves and therefore narratives.

22. MWO to James Weldon Johnson, 24 October 1929, James Weldon Johnson Collection, Yale University.

23. Jane Addams, Preface, *Twenty Years at Hull-House,* xvii–xviii. Parts of Addams's book were also first published in periodicals: *McClure's Magazine* and *The American Magazine.* Addams's autobiographical text, even with its stated goal, contains more internal material than does Ovington's. It has thus lent itself to analysis on questions of self and form in such articles as

Rebecca Sherrick, "Their Fathers' Daughters: The Autobiographies of Jane Addams and Florence Kelly," *American Studies* 27 (Spring 1986): 39–53; and Debra Holding, "The Body of Work: Illness as Narrative Strategy in Jane Addams' *Twenty Years at Hull-House*," *A/B: Auto/Biography Studies* 6 (Spring 1991): 33–39.

24. Jill Ker Conway, ed., *Written by Herself: Autobiographies of American Women: An Anthology* (New York: Vintage, 1992), ix–xi and 471–73.

25. Friedman, "Women's Autobiographical Selves," *The Private Self*, 34–62.

26. For these women's autobiographical texts about settlement work, see Simkhovitch, *Neighborhood: My Story of Greenwich House* (New York: W. W. Norton, 1938), and Wald, *The House on Henry Street* (New York: Henry Holt and Company, 1915) and *Windows on Henry Street* (Boston: Little, Brown and Company, 1934).

27. See, for example, Sidonie Smith, *A Poetics of Women's Autobiography: Marginality and the Fictions of Self-Representation* (Bloomington and Indianapolis: Indiana University Press, 1987), 4–5; James Olney, "Autobiography and the Cultural Moment: A Thematic, Historical, and Bibliographical Introduction," *Autobiography: Essays Theoretical and Critical*, James Olney, ed. (Princeton: Princeton University Press, 1980), 3–27.

28. "Choosing Sides, Choosing Lives: Women's Autobiographies of the Civil Rights Movement," *American Women's Autobiography: Fea(s)ts of Memory*, Margo Culley, ed. (Madison: University of Wisconsin Press, 1992), 228.

Top: Walter White (left),
Mary White Ovington, (second from
left), William Pickens (third from right),
and Arthur Spingarn (right) led the
NAACP when Ovington penned her
reminiscences.

Right: Frederick Douglass, the noted
abolitionist lecturer, in his final years.

Top: Mary White Ovington in her later years.

Top right: Walter White succeeded James Weldon Johnson as the Executive Secretary of the NAACP.

Facing page, top left: Booker T. Washington, the Principal of Tuskegee Institute.

Facing page, top right: Carl Murphy, the editor of the Baltimore Afro-American, offered to publish Ovington's reminiscences for his readers.

Facing page, center left: Mary Church Terrell was the founding President of the National Association of Colored Women.

Facing page, center right: W.E.B. Du Bois, the NAACP's first Director of Publicity and Research, who "wanted from the white man something more than money," Ovington recalled. He wanted "a state of mind." (Archives, University Library, University of Massachusetts, Amherst)

Facing page, bottom right: Ida B. Wells, who crusaded against lynching for years before the NAACP was organized. (Special Collections, Joseph Regenstein Library, University of Chicago)

Except where noted, all photographs are courtesy of the Photographs and Prints Division, Schomburg Center for Research in Black Culture, The New York Public Library, Astor, Lenox and Tilden Foundations.

The *Feminist Press at The City University of New York* offers alternatives in education and in literature. Founded in 1970, this nonprofit, tax-exempt educational and publishing organization works to eliminate stereotypes in books and schools and to provide literature with a broad vision of human potential. The publishing program includes reprints of important works by women, feminist biographies of women, multicultural anthologies, a cross-cultural memoir series, and nonsexist children's books. Curricular materials, bibliographies, directories, and a quarterly journal provide information and support for students and teachers of women's studies. Through publications and projects, The Feminist Press contributes to the rediscovery of the history of women and the emergence of a more humane society.

New and Forthcoming Books

The Answer/La Respuesta (Including a Selection of Poems), by Sor Juana Inés de la Cruz. Critical edition and translation by Electa Arenal and Amanda Powell. $12.95 paper, $35.00 cloth.

Australia for Women: Travel and Culture, edited by Susan Hawthorne and Renate Klein. $17.95 paper.

The Castle of Pictures and Other Stories: A Grandmother's Tales, Volume One, by George Sand. Edited and translated by Holly Erskine Hirko. Illustrated by Mary Warshaw. $9.95 paper, $19.95 cloth.

Challenging Racism and Sexism: Alternatives to Genetic Explanations (Genes & Gender VII), edited by Ethel Tobach and Betty Rosoff. $14.95 paper, $35.00 cloth.

Folly, a novel by Maureen Brady. Afterword by Bonnie Zimmerman. $12.95 paper, $35.00 cloth.

Japanese Women: New Feminist Perspectives on the Past, Present, and Future, edited by Kumiko Fujimura-Fanselow and Atsuko Kameda. $15.95 paper, $35.00 cloth.

Shedding and Literally Dreaming, by Verena Stefan. Afterword by Tobe Levin. $14.95 paper, $35.00 cloth.

The Slate of Life: More Contemporary Stories by Women Writers of India, edited by Kali for Women. Introduction by Chandra Talpade Mohanty and Satya P. Mohanty. $12.95 paper, $35.00 cloth.

Songs My Mother Taught Me: Stories, Plays, and Memoir, by Wakako Yamauchi. Edited and with an introduction by Garrett Hongo. Afterword by Valerie Miner. $14.95 paper, $35.00 cloth.

Women of Color and the Multicultural Curriculum: Transforming the College Classroom, edited by Liza Fiol-Matta and Mariam K. Chamberlain. $18.95 paper, $35.00 cloth.

Prices subject to change. *Individuals:* Send check or money order (in U.S. dollars drawn on a U.S. bank) to The Feminist Press at The City University of New York, 311 East 94th Street, New York, NY 10128. Please include $4.00 postage and handling for the first book, $1.00 for each additional. For VISA/MasterCard orders call (212) 360- 5790. *Bookstores, libraries, wholesalers:* Feminist Press titles are distributed to the trade by Consortium Book Sales and Distribution, (800) 283- 3572.

7223